PLACES AND CASES

Europe

John Edwards

Series Editor
Peter Webber

Stanley Thornes (Publishers) Ltd

Text © John Edwards 1998

Original line illustrations © Stanley Thornes (Publishers) Ltd 1998

Designed by Peter Tucker, Holbrook Design (Oxford) Ltd
Illustrated by Tim Smith and Hardlines
Cover photo: Science Photo Library
Picture research by Penni Bickle

The right of John Edwards to be identified as author of this work has been asserted by him in accordance with the Copyright, Designs and Patents Act 1988.

First published in 1998 by:
Stanley Thornes (Publishers) Ltd
Ellenborough House
Wellington Street
CHELTENHAM GL50 1YW
England

98 99 00 01 02 / 10 9 8 7 6 5 4 3 2 1

A catalogue record for this book is available from the British Library.

ISBN 0-7487-2916-X

Printed and bound in Italy by STIGE, Turin

Acknowledgements
With thanks to the following for permission to reproduce photographs and other copyright material in this book:

Penni Bickle, 90H; Sylvia Cordaiy, 21 (top); James Davis Travel Photography, 19G, 35H, 41F; Ecoscene, 84B (bottom); Eye Ubiquitous, 15A (bottom), 24G (right), 61B, 62C, 92E (right); Fiat UK Ltd, 55C; Lesley Garland Picture Library, 10G, 15A (top right), 23C; Gateway 2000, 48D; Getty Images, 13L, 32B (left and right), 51A, 72D, 77B, 88D (top); Greenpeace/Sims, 44D; Impact Photos, 15A (left), 26B, 44C, 65F (right), 87A (right), 91B; Science Photo Library, 13M, 42I; Still Pictures, 16B, 82H (top); Topham Picturepoint, 21 (left), 31L, 34E (left and right), 40E, 68L (bottom), 80E (bottom), 87A (left); Trip Photographic Library, 9B, 11D, 18F, 21 (right), 24G (left), 28E, 47B, 51B, 59E, 64E (top and bottom), 68L (top), 70N, 75G and H, 76A (top and bottom), 79B and C, 80E (top), 82H (bottom), 84B (top), 86F, 88D (bottom), 92D and E (left).

All other photographs by John Edwards.

Wolters-Noordhoff, 30I & K; Topografische Dienst, the Netherlands, 31M; Michelin, from map 83, 27th Edition, 1998. Authorisation no. 9801012, 34F; Falk-Verlag AG © Kartographie: Geo Data, 40D; Motorola, 49E; Trinity College Dublin, 50G; Fiat Group, UK, 54–56; Collins-Longman Atlases, 58D; Telegraph Group Limited, 1997, 72C.

Every effort has been made to contact copyright holders. The publishers apologise to anyone whose rights have been inadvertently overlooked, and will be happy to rectify any errors or omissions.

Contents

Introduction

To the student

This book about Europe is one in a series of three textbooks for GCSE Geography. One book covers the United Kingdom, while a third looks at world-wide issues.

You will find that much of the book consists of case studies. There is some background information about a topic before many of the case studies are introduced. For example, the case study on page 9 examines Sweden in the north of Europe. Before the case study, the materials get you to think about the climate and physical landscape. However, if you are able to make the best of the case study, you need to have ideas already about the geography of Europe. This is why there is a 'Do you know?' box at the start of each unit. It is assumed that you use a 'core' geography textbook and will have had some class time to make sure you know the definitions and the answers to any questions in the 'Do you know?' box before you study the topics in this book. This case study approach allows you to deepen and broaden your knowledge and understanding.

The case studies have been chosen to cover the main topics you need for your GCSE syllabuses. So, you will find case studies on earthquakes, ecosystems, weather and climate, population, settlement, development and environmental issues. Most GCSE examinations either include case studies for you to analyse, or ask you to use a case study you have studied. This book, therefore, gives you practice and examples. You will find that the activities throughout the book will help you develop the different skills you need in examinations. These include using photographs, tables, graphs, maps, diagrams, charts, as well as reading sections of text and completing decision making exercises. This book gives you plenty of practice!

The symbol ➡ suggests that you write at greater length and in more detail. Your answer should be at least a paragraph in length.

Some of the words which appear in bold throughout this book are key terms which are defined in the Glossary on page 96.

The value of currency in European countries is often measured in US dollars, to allow comparison between different currencies. In some cases figures are given in ECUs. This is the European Currency Unit, to be used by all countries joining the European Union's single currency.

Geography is all about how the world works – the natural world and the human world – and is about more than examinations. So, we hope this book will help you to take an interest in and begin to understand the world around you.

Enjoy your Geography!

Political map of Europe

It is difficult to define the exact boundaries of Europe. Recent political changes have seen the number of European states increase, together with the dominance of the European Union. The turmoil following the collapse of communism in eastern Europe has blurred some divisions, while creating others.

This book takes its case studies from throughout Europe. Many of the more familiar studies are from western Europe, those less familiar are from the east. The maps in this section locate the main case studies used elsewhere in the book. Reference is made throughout to the United Kingdom, as a part of Europe. Figure A shows the current state of Europe's ever-changing political geography. Before going any further, think about where you would draw the boundaries of Europe. What makes a country 'European'? Is it the type of language spoken, membership of institutions like the European Union, or perhaps participation in the Eurovision Song Contest?

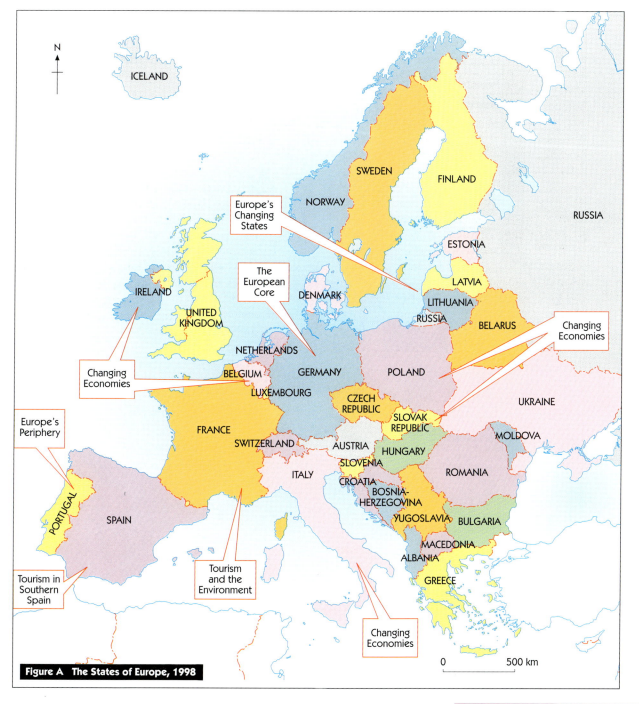

Figure A The States of Europe, 1998

Europe's climates

Figure B shows the main climates to be found in Europe. As the map and climate graphs show, there is an enormous variety of climates to be found in the continent. Climate is important in the effects it has upon people's everyday lives, and also on the economy of a country.

We expect the climate of Moscow and London to be different, as we do that of Rome and Tromso. Sometimes these differences are great, yet there are surprising similarities. Russia has much more severe winters than England, but the summer maximum temperatures for London and Moscow are the same. A summer holiday in Italy would be much warmer than in northern Norway, while there is relatively little difference between Rome and Tromso in terms of annual precipitation.

The importance of climate upon human activity is apparent in case studies throughout the book. Figure B refers to some of these examples.

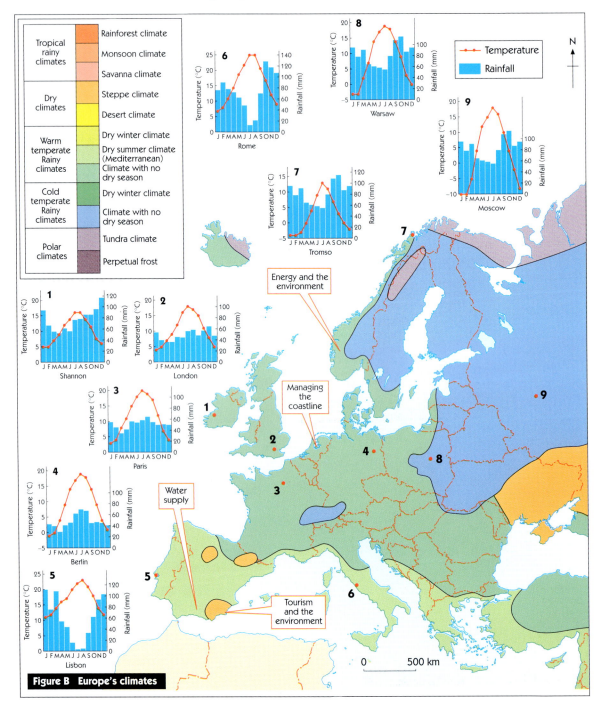

Figure B Europe's climates

The physical environment

The nature of the physical environment can have an important impact upon human activity. In addition to the effects of climate, relief and landforms affect the location of settlements, the nature of economic activity and the effectiveness of transport links. The importance of the physical environment is apparent across Europe and is illustrated through the case studies shown in Figure C.

The Scandinavian north of Europe has been influenced by past Ice Ages. The mountains of the north of Europe rise to over 2,400 metres, are flat topped and cut by deep glaciated valleys. These are flooded at the coast to form fjords. Central Europe consists of a mixture of broad uplands (about 1,000 metres) and vast lowland areas. The south and east of the continent are characterised by high mountain ranges separated by wide plains, for example, the Alps and the Pyrenees.

The favourable physical environment of much of Europe has encouraged settlement and the varied relief has encouraged growth in the major plains and valleys. Even the mountains, with hostile environments, have not escaped human influence. Only the frozen wastes of northern Scandinavia remain virtually unpopulated.

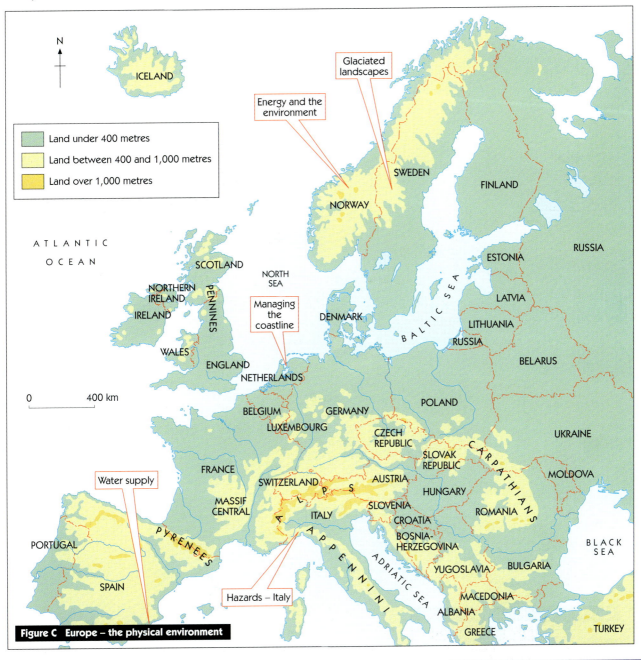

Figure C Europe – the physical environment

Population distribution

The population of Europe is distributed unevenly, as shown by Figure D. Population density varies on a regional as well as a national scale. South-east England, for example, is much more densely inhabited than any other part of the United Kingdom. Although densities in Scandinavia are generally low, Stockholm and Copenhagen are examples of local centres of high population density.

The distribution of Europe's population owes much to the nature of the physical environment (see page 7). The low-lying, mild and fertile areas stretching from England to Germany have some of the greatest concentrations of people.

On the other hand, the harsh terrain and inhospitable climate of northern Scandinavia have discouraged most settlers. However, even in sparsely populated regions local concentrations emerge. Some of Europe's capital cities, for example Madrid and Dublin, are in regions of relatively low population. **The photograph on the front cover shows Europe at night. Compare this with Figure D**. The lights of Europe show how people have spread to every corner of the continent, and suggest that further population growth in the twenty-first century will put increasing pressure upon already limited space.

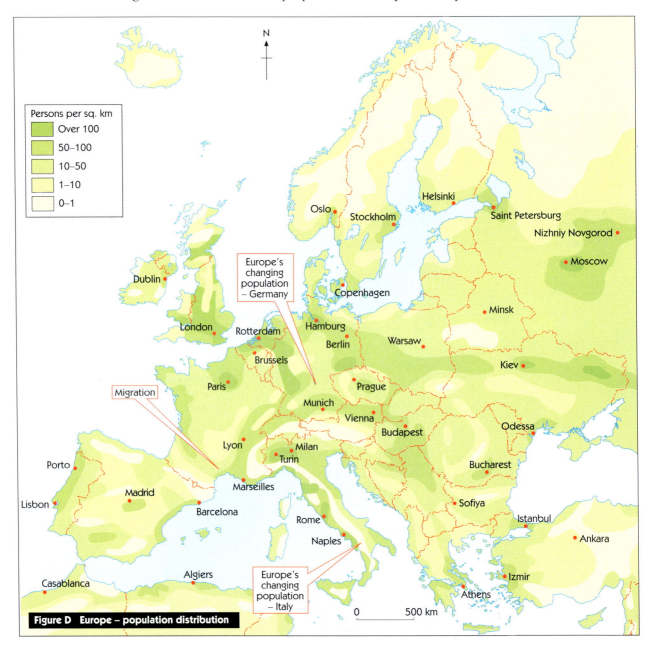

Figure D   Europe – population distribution

Persons per sq. km
- Over 100
- 50–100
- 10–50
- 1–10
- 0–1

Europe's landscapes

The variety of physical landscapes that make up the continent of Europe are shown on page 7. From the north of Scandinavia to the south of Italy, the natural environment has an influence on human activity. The countries of Sweden and Italy illustrate the effects of the environment, how it may be used as a resource and the need for conservation.

(see page 7)

Key ideas & questions

● The physical environment can be a resource as well as a hazard.
● In what ways have physical landforms in Sweden and Italy affected human activity?

Main activity

Resource questions on Swedish landscapes and Mount Etna, Sicily.

Do you know?

? The coastline of Sweden is over 6,000km in length.
? One-seventh of Sweden is within the Arctic Circle, receiving about two months of continual darkness in the winter.
? Sicily is the largest island in the Mediterranean Sea. In addition to being the location of Europe's largest active volcano, the area is also in an earthquake zone.
? There have been over 90 recorded eruptions of Mount Etna. The most disastrous of these was in 1669, when more than 20,000 people were killed.

CASE STUDY: The European north – Sweden

Sweden is the third largest country in Europe, stretching 1,400km from north to south (see Figure A). The country is situated on roughly the same latitude as Alaska and Siberia, yet in much of Sweden the climate is relatively mild. This is due to the influence of the Gulf Stream, which carries warm water across the Atlantic Ocean from the Caribbean, warming Scandinavia's extensive coastline. Although climate has an important influence on the human geography of Sweden, it is the physical geography of the country which has dominated the settlement pattern and economy of Sweden.

Figure B Almost all of Sweden's farmland is in the south of the country

Figure A   The location of Sweden

The southern part of the country is a continuation of the fertile plains of Denmark and northern Germany. Here, wide plains make up most of the 9 % of Sweden which is farmed (see Figure B). The rest of southern Sweden is a mixture of undulating hills, fields and lakes. The north of the country is dominated by mountains formed mostly from **granite** and **gneiss** (igneous and metamorphic rocks, see Figure C). These vast highlands, ranging from 1,000 to 2,000 metres above sea level, contain much of Sweden's forests and are cut by its largest rivers.

Figure C Snowmelt in the mountains of Lapland, northern Sweden

Earth movements millions of years ago (during the Tertiary Period) have given Sweden its characteristic relief. However, events more recent in geological history have also left their mark on the landscape. During periods of colder climate, Scandinavia has been covered by ice. The most recent Ice Age ended only about 10,000 years ago. The weight and movement of the ice sheet, several kilometres thick in places, altered the landscape beneath.

Everywhere in Sweden shows the effects of glaciation. The hard rocks of the northern mountains were rounded and polished by the ice, and hollows and valleys deepened and widened. In the south there is finely ground glacial and **fluvio-glacial material**. This sank slowly to the sea bottom at the edge of the ice mass, later to be raised to form the fertile soils of the southern lowlands.

The ice mass was so heavy that it actually depressed the level of land underneath. Since the ice retreated 10,000 years ago, the Scandinavian peninsula has been rising from the sea again. Today, Sweden is still in the process of regaining the land contours it had before glaciation. The northern part of the country is rising at a rate of about one centimetre per year, the southern part one millimetre. This rising of the land is set to continue for thousands of years to come. The Gulf of Bothnia, the northern part of the Baltic Sea, could eventually be raised above sea level.

When the inland ice finally melted away about 8,000 years ago, it left behind irregularities in the ground that quickly became filled with water. The retreating ice left about 100,000 such hollows, making Sweden one of the countries in the world richest in lakes.

Today, the rivers flowing south-east from Sweden's highlands form one of its most important resources. Sweden is Europe's third greatest consumer of **hydro-electric power**, behind Norway and France (see also pages 22–25). All but three of the country's large rivers have HEP schemes, contributing 16 % of Sweden's energy consumption.

Since the end of the Ice Age, Sweden has been a country dominated by forests (see Figure D). Over half of the country is forested, providing an economic and recreational resource. The south of Sweden is dominated by deciduous trees such as birch, while the north is home to vast areas of pine and spruce.

Figure D Forests dominate landscapes throughout Sweden and are an important natural resource

law in a number of different ways. There are 26 National Parks within the country where no commercial use of land is permitted (see Figure E). The mountains make up 90 % of the area of the National Parks, which preserve the unique character of Sweden's natural landscape. Smaller areas are protected as nature reserves. The 1,600 Swedish reserves are mostly small and near to settlements, which allows for their use as leisure resources. The Lapland mountains in the north of Sweden are on the United Nations' World Heritage list. The areas on the World Heritage list are considered to be of such importance that their conservation is a concern for the whole of humanity.

As a result, Sweden's population is distributed very unevenly. A population of nine million people occupy 450,000 square kilometres, an average of 20 people per square kilometre. A third of Sweden's population live in the cities of Stockholm, Malmö and Göteborg (see Figure A) and along the Baltic coastline to the north of Stockholm. Only 20 % of the population live in Norrland, the northern two thirds of the country. Here, population density is only two people per square kilometre, compared with nearly 300 in Stockholm.

The untouched character of Sweden's mountain landscapes is under increasing threat. The expansion of hydro-electric power, mining, roads and tourist facilities has already invaded the wilderness. New types of mountain tourism, such as pony trekking or mountain bike riding, increase deposits of rubbish and cause wear and tear in the sensitive environment. Forestry is also threatening the stability of the natural environment. Many plants and insects, which provide food for birds and animals, need the dead wood of rotting trees for their survival. Sweden's main export earning industry has reduced the range of life in the forests.

Sweden's natural environment is protected by

Vadvetjåkka
Abisko
Stora sjöfallet
Kiruna
Padjelanta
Muddus
Sarek
Arctic circle
Pieljekaise
Luleå
Haparanda Sandskär
Björnlandet
Umeå
Sånfjället
Skuleskogen
Töfsingdalen
Hamra
Färnebofjärden
Garphyttan
Ängsö
Tresticklan
Stockholm
Djurö
Tyresta
Norra Kvill
Tiveden
Gotska Sandön
Göteborg
Store Mosse
Blå Jungfrun
Öland
Dalby Söderskog
Malmö
Stenshuvud

N

0   300 km

Figure E   Sweden's National Parks

Italy lies near to the southern edge of the Eurasian Plate and its border with the African Plate. In such a location, Italy is prone to the earthquakes and volcanic activity caused by the movement of the Earth's crustal plates. The physical environment may be seen as a hazard; earthquakes have hit all parts of the country, while the southern part of Italy has active volcanoes (see Figure F).

Volcanic landscapes may also be a resource. As well as providing good quality soils, Italy's volcanoes are an attraction to many tourists. Vesuvius, near the city of Naples, is a famous example.

Mount Etna

Mount Etna, on the island of Sicily, is one of Europe's most active volcanoes. The vast volcanic cone dominates the eastern side of the island, reaching over 3,300 metres above sea level (see Figures G and H). The satellite photograph, Figure I, shows the eastern part of Sicily together with the southern tip of the Italian mainland. The dark volcanic cone of Mount Etna is clearly visible near the east coast of the island.

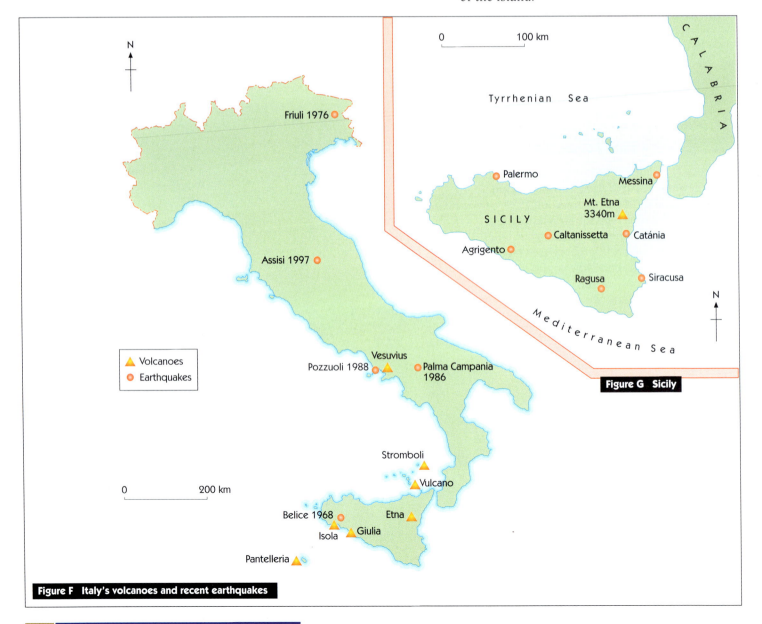

Figure G Sicily

Figure F Italy's volcanoes and recent earthquakes

Figure H   Mount Etna

As an active volcano, Etna poses a continual threat to inhabitants of the local area. The higher parts of the mountain are covered in snow for most of the year, but lower forested slopes provide rich fertile volcanic soils (see Figure J). These are a contrast to poor quality land found in other parts of Sicily, and attract people to the area despite the dangers of further eruptions.

Figure I   Satellite image of Sicily

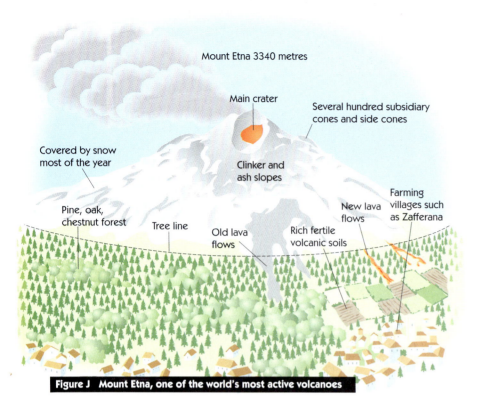

Figure J   Mount Etna, one of the world's most active volcanoes

Labels on figure:
- Mount Etna 3340 metres
- Main crater
- Several hundred subsidiary cones and side cones
- Covered by snow most of the year
- Clinker and ash slopes
- Pine, oak, chestnut forest
- Tree line
- Old lava flows
- Rich fertile volcanic soils
- New lava flows
- Farming villages such as Zafferana

A report of the 1992 eruption of Mount Etna describes how the local population tried to deal with the hazard.

An international television audience watched as helicopters dropped blocks of concrete onto a lava flow to change its direction. The lava flow was coming from yet another eruption of Mount Etna in Sicily. The concrete blocks formed a dam to protect the village of Zafferana, which has a population of 5,000. The dam only held for 23 days and the lava spilled over the top to threaten the village once again. In another attempt to fight the giant volcano the army used explosives to divert the lava flow.

But science and engineering could not save farmland, tracks, houses and barns. Local beekeeper Pietro Lafata said 'I'm not afraid of lava – it never kills anyone. We're used to eruptions here. They happen all the time. Mind you, I'm scared I might lose my house. Still, we cannot fight it. We must respect nature. Etna, she is the boss.'

Other villagers believed in the power of prayer and showed off the Virgin's shrine which the magma flow stopped short of engulfing 200 years earlier. Many inhabitants of Zafferana had lived with the volcanic threat all their lives. Etna is 3,340 metres high and nearly 160 kilometres around its base. They really did not think they would be affected by the occasional lava flow. They earned their living from farming the slopes of Etna and from the tourists who visited the volcano which erupted every six or seven years.

▼ Questions

1 Describe the main physical landscapes of Sweden. Use the information on page 7 to help you.
2 How have these landscapes affected people?
3 What has been done to preserve the natural landscapes of Sweden?
4 Read through the opinions below, which are from people involved with the development and protection of Sweden's forests.

a 'Forestry is an industry, just like any other. As long as we make money from the trees we grow, what does it matter if the number of types of plants and animals in the forest goes down?'

b 'Many insects and plants will become extinct in Sweden if forestry methods do not change. Tree felling must be banned from the most threatened areas. If this means that companies make less profit, so be it. Plants, insects and animals dying out will affect us all in the end.'

What do you think of these opinions? Write a detailed comment about each of them.➡

5 Find out about an industry or company which has an effect on the natural environment. What has been done to conserve the natural environment?
6 Describe and give reasons for the location of Italy's volcanoes and earthquakes.
7 Draw a sketch of Mount Etna based on Figure J. Add labels to your diagram to describe what happened during the eruption of 1992.
8 Describe the attempts made to stop the lava flows. What is your opinion of the attitudes of local people to the volcano? In what ways is Etna a hazard as well as a resource?➡

Review

The variety of landscapes in Europe have an impact upon human activity. Some natural environments may be a resource as well as a hazard. Sweden, in the north of Europe, shows the effects of recent Ice Ages. The rivers and lakes left after the glaciers retreated, together with immense forests, are the country's greatest natural resources. Italy, in the south of Europe, is affected by volcanoes and earthquakes. Although a hazard, people live near volcanoes, such as Mount Etna, as they provide fertile soil for farmers. Volcanoes are also a tourist attraction.

2

Water supply

Key ideas & questions

- A clean water supply is fundamental to human life.
- The provision of a regular supply of water has a major impact on people's activities, and needs careful management.
- How does Spain cope with the problems of providing fresh water?

Main activity

Response questions and comparison work.

The total quantity of water available to the people of Europe is limited. More people are making more demands upon fresh water supplies, leading to increasing strain upon this most precious natural resource. On a global scale, agriculture accounts for the majority of water consumption, although this is not the case in Europe (see Figure A). Domestic water use is only a small part of the total, but is often the most costly to provide. The quality of water needed in the home is higher than that needed for industry or farming. The technology needed to ensure that our drinking water is free from contamination is expensive.

Water supply

Water, unlike other resources, cannot easily be transported from one part of the world to another. Reservoirs and pipelines carry water over relatively long distances, but these are solutions only to regional problems, often within one country. The transfer of water is costly, and often underground stores of water are tapped instead. These supplies are limited, and many are being depleted faster than they are being renewed. The pollution of water sources is a major problem in many parts of Europe. In the former Soviet Union, for example, the lack of environmental controls on industry has led to 75 % of surface water being unfit to drink.

The availability of fresh water varies greatly across Europe. The north of the continent is generally wetter than the south, where rainfall also tends to be seasonal and unreliable. The water balance (see Figure C) shows that it is the countries of southern Europe that are most likely to experience problems providing fresh water. Some of the poorest parts of Europe suffer from drought, and the provision of a reliable supply of fresh water is essential for their economic development.

Do you know?

? The population of the world is seven times greater than 300 years ago. Water use has increased by 35 times during the same period.
? In the last 40 years, the amount of fresh water available per person in the world has halved.

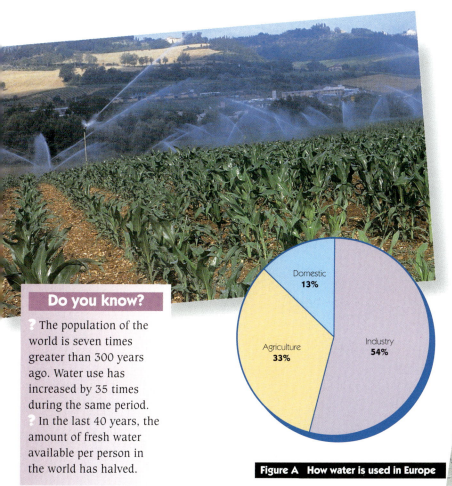

Figure A   How water is used in Europe

Domestic 13% / Agriculture 33% / Industry 54%

CASE STUDY: Supplying Spain's water

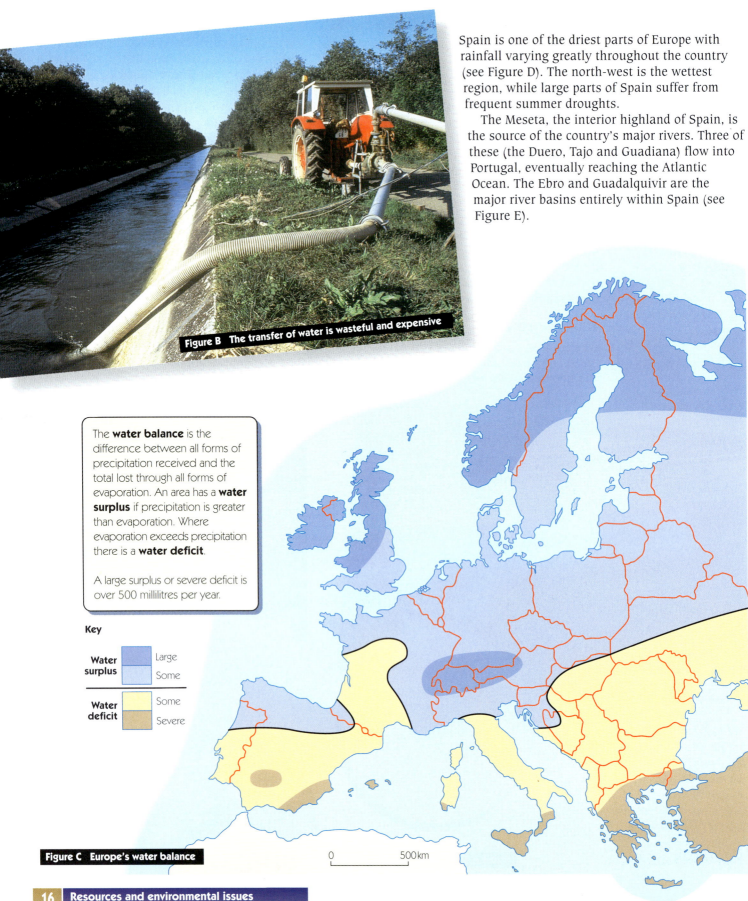

Figure B The transfer of water is wasteful and expensive

Spain is one of the driest parts of Europe with rainfall varying greatly throughout the country (see Figure D). The north-west is the wettest region, while large parts of Spain suffer from frequent summer droughts.

The Meseta, the interior highland of Spain, is the source of the country's major rivers. Three of these (the Duero, Tajo and Guadiana) flow into Portugal, eventually reaching the Atlantic Ocean. The Ebro and Guadalquivir are the major river basins entirely within Spain (see Figure E).

The **water balance** is the difference between all forms of precipitation received and the total lost through all forms of evaporation. An area has a **water surplus** if precipitation is greater than evaporation. Where evaporation exceeds precipitation there is a **water deficit**.

A large surplus or severe deficit is over 500 millilitres per year.

Key

Water surplus
- Large
- Some

Water deficit
- Some
- Severe

Figure C Europe's water balance

0   500km

The Spanish national water authority has the responsibility of maintaining the country's fresh water supply. The authority is faced with a series of problems:

● Much of Spain experiences a water deficit, with demand being greater than supply.

● Throughout most of the interior and south of Spain, rainfall is unreliable and droughts are common.

● Evaporation rates are greater than precipitation, making the storage of water difficult.

● Agriculture needs water for only a few months of the year, but peak demands are during parts of the year when rainfall is at its lowest.

● Tourism has increased the pressure on water resources. Tourists use far more water than local people, once again in the months when there is least rainfall.

● The greatest tourist demand is in coastal regions, where underground water is used as well as rainfall. This limited supply of water is being used up far more quickly than it is naturally being replaced.

In many cases, the Spanish authorities have built large dams to store water for times of greatest demand. Madrid, for example, is ringed by 26 reservoirs. Water is brought to the people of the city by an extensive canal system. The use of ground water supplies has become common to maintain supplies, and in the short term has proved an effective solution. Where demand still exceeds supply, water has been transferred from wetter regions.

Problems

These solutions have brought problems of their own. The driest parts of Spain suffer from soil erosion, producing sediment which gets trapped behind dams. This causes increased pressure on the structure of the dam, and reduces the storage capacity of the reservoir. With high rates of evaporation, salts concentrate in reservoir waters, serving as nutrients for the growth of algae. This process of **eutrophication** has become a problem in many arid regions. The greatest use of underground water is in coastal regions, to meet tourist demands. This has led to the contamination of fresh water supplies by sea water, and damaged natural environments (see Andalusia on page 18).

Solutions

The Spanish government is trying to find ways to meet the ever increasing demand for water. More efficient methods of irrigation could greatly reduce the amount of water wasted through agricultural use. Another possibility involves developing crops which have lower water requirements, growing when rainfall levels are highest during the year.

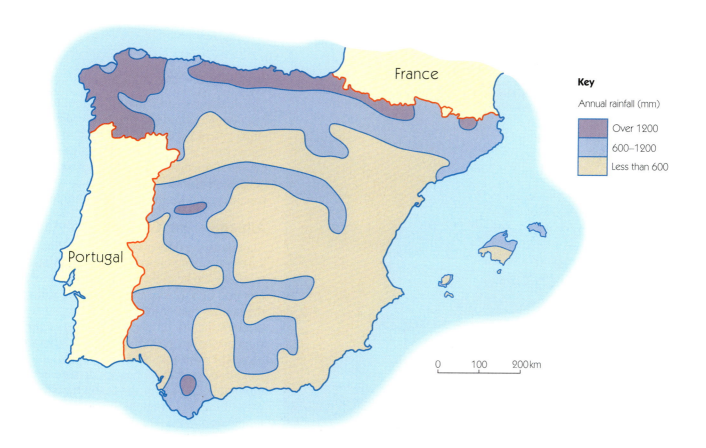

Key

Annual rainfall (mm)

Over 1200

600–1200

Less than 600

Figure D   The rain in Spain...

Figure E Spain's five major river basins

Figure F Almeria is Europe's only desert region

Andalusia – the arid south

Andalusia is Spain's poorest region. It relies heavily upon tourism, which provides employment for 60 % of the working population. Agriculture is the region's next highest earner. Levels of unemployment are high and economic development has often taken place with little consideration for the natural environment.

Almeria – the 'Costa del Polythene'

Almeria is the only place in Europe classified as a desert, having on average less than 16 cm of rainfall each year (see Figure F). Until recently, this arid area was of little economic value. In the last 20 years Almeria has been transformed through the use of irrigation. Water is pumped from below the surface in order to supply the area. The advantages of this method of irrigation are that it does not depend upon unreliable rainfall, or the costly transfer of water from other regions. There are, however, problems as well. The amount of ground water available is limited, and supplies are being rapidly depleted. This over-use has lowered the water table, drawing in sea water which

Figure G   Plastic greenhouses in the Almeria region known as the 'Costa del polythene'

contaminates the water used for irrigation (see Figure H).

The management of Almeria's water supply has seen the area grow into Europe's most important centre for greenhouse cultivation. Over 10,000 hectares of plastic greenhouses produce 250 million kilograms of greenhouse crops per year (see Figure G). Tomatoes, melons, courgettes and peppers are exported to other European countries, especially when out of season in northern Europe. These greenhouse crops have had a major impact on Almeria, and on Andalusia as a whole. They have made an important contribution to the economy of one of the poorest parts of Spain. In the driest part of Europe demand for water exceeds supply. The amount and quality of available ground water is in decline due to the growth in demand for water for agriculture. Irrigation is an inefficient user of precious water supplies, much water is lost due to seepage into the soil, or because of high rates of evaporation. The greenhouses are considered by many to be a visual blot on the landscape, with environmental problems outweighing the economic benefits brought to the region.

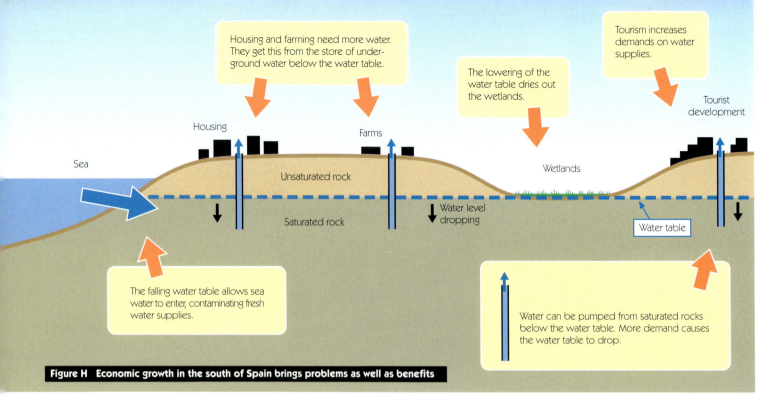

Housing and farming need more water. They get this from the store of underground water below the water table.

The lowering of the water table dries out the wetlands.

Tourism increases demands on water supplies.

Tourist development

Housing

Farms

Sea

Unsaturated rock

Wetlands

Saturated rock

Water level dropping

Water table

The falling water table allows sea water to enter, contaminating fresh water supplies.

Water can be pumped from saturated rocks below the water table. More demand causes the water table to drop.

Figure H   Economic growth in the south of Spain brings problems as well as benefits

The Guadalquivir – conflicting demands

Tourism and agriculture, Andalusia's main industries, make different demands upon the natural environment. In some cases, these may conflict with each other, and frequently they both cause problems for conservation of the environment.

The river Guadalquivir reaches the Atlantic Ocean to the south of the city of Seville (see Figure J). The mouth of the river forms a wetland, called the Coto de Donana. For many years, this **wetland** has been famous for its natural flora and fauna, rather like the **Camargue** in France (see pages 33–37). The area was designated a National Park in 1969 in order to help preserve some of the rare **species** of plants and animals present.

In recent years the natural environment has come under increasing threat from agriculture and tourism. With little rainfall, farmers use water stored underground to irrigate their crops. Irrigation is very wasteful and expensive, and the use of underground water has caused the same sea water contamination problems as at Almeria. The wetland is drying out as more and more water is used for rice cultivation. In order to increase crop yields farmers have used fertilisers and pesticides, which have led to further problems.

Tourism is the most important growth industry in Andalusia. More tourists would bring increased revenue into an area of high unemployment and low paid jobs. Yet, holiday developments have a visual impact on the environment and tourism increases other forms of pollution as well. The water requirements of holidaymakers would drain the wetlands of the Coto de Donana and destroy the natural habitat of many rare species of wildlife, e.g. the purple heron. If the wetland disappears then the area loses one of its tourist resources.

Water supply in the future

It is likely that Europe's water resource problems will become more acute in the future. An increasing population will demand more water, for both domestic and commercial purposes. In response to this, more water will have to be taken from underground sources, making the sustainable use of water supplies even more difficult. A lowering of the water table would make removal of water more expensive, and reduce the occurrence of springs and streams. In coastal areas the problem of contamination by salt water could be made worse by the rise in sea level predicted by many experts. The transfer of water over long distances remains a costly alternative, although used increasingly in Europe.

Global climate change could have an important, if unpredictable, effect upon water supply. Forecasts based on a temperature rise of 1–2 °C, with a 10 % reduction in rainfall could result in a halving of underground water supplies. Less rainfall could lead to the spread of **desertification** through fragile environments in southern Europe. The management of water supplies is likely to become an issue of ever increasing importance throughout the continent in the twenty-first century.

0   100km

Figure J The river Guadalquivir

Cordoba

R.Guadalquivir

SEVILLE

Coto de Donana National Park

Almeria

Malaga

Cadiz

Mediterranean Sea

Atlantic Ocean

The Guadalquivir is home to many species of wildlife

Farming makes increased demands on the land

Tourism brings added pressures as well as benefits

▼ Questions

1 What are the main uses of water on a global scale? Give an example of each.

2 Why is domestic water supply (i.e. for homes) so costly?

3 Which areas of Europe have:
   a   a deficit in water supply;
   b   a surplus in water supply?
   Why is this?

4 What are the problems faced by Spain in trying to provide a fresh water supply for the whole of the country? You should refer to the climate map on page 6 to help you with your answer.

5 How have the Spanish authorities attempted to solve these problems?

6 Using Almeria as an example, what are the advantages and disadvantages of economic development in a poor region? ➔

7 What are the similarities and differences between the Coto de Donana in Spain and the Camargue in France? (see pages 33–37). ➔

Review

The availability of fresh water varies throughout Europe, with the north of the continent being wetter than the south. Many countries in the south of Europe experience water shortages. Dams are used to store water for times of deficit, and underground stores of water are used. Each of these brings its own problems.

Spain is one of the driest countries in Europe, with the south in particular experiencing frequent shortages. Demand is increasing as agriculture and tourist developments bring more jobs to the region. Different land uses often conflict, and the natural environment may be damaged. The supply of fresh water is likely to become an increasing problem in the future, particularly for countries in the south of Europe.

Energy and the environment

Key ideas & questions

- Energy use is closely linked to economic development. It can also seriously affect the physical environment.
- How has the development of energy sources in Norway affected the economy and the physical environment of the country?
- What conflicts have developed between damage to the environment and the creation of wealth and job opportunities in Norway?

Main activity

Assessing the economic gains and environmental losses of the Norwegian energy industry.

Europe produces nearly half of the energy that it consumes. The amount produced varies from one country to another, and the level of dependence on imports is decreasing. The Netherlands, for example, is an overall exporter of energy. This is due largely to the country's huge reserves of natural gas. Other countries such as France and Belgium have turned to nuclear power to meet their energy needs. Portugal, on the other hand, is an example of a country that still relies heavily upon imports, 97 % of its requirements come from abroad.

CASE STUDY: Energy and development in Norway

Nowhere in Norway is far from the sea. The country has the longest coastline in Europe, with a third of its land being within the Arctic Circle (see Figure A). Norway is a mountainous country, dominated by highlands usually 500–800 metres above sea level. The highest parts of the country still have permanent ice fields. In the east of Norway the highlands are broken by deep valleys flowing to the lowlands of the south-east of the country. With so much barren and inaccessible land, only 2 % of Norway is farmed.

Everywhere, fishing is an important industry. Forestry, chemical and metal industries are important, but it is the development of Norway's energy sources which has transformed the economy of the country in recent years. Oil, gas and hydro-electric power (HEP) have enabled rapid industrial development. Norway boasts one of the highest levels of Gross National Product (GNP) in Europe, see Figure B.

Do you know?

? Oil is the world's most important fuel, accounting for 40 % of energy used.

? At current production rates, the world's known oil reserves will last for only 40 years.

? Nuclear power now represents 7.2 % of world energy production, more than ever before.

? The United States is responsible for 25 % of global energy consumption.

Figure A   The location of Norway

Country: Kingdom of Norway

Area:	323,900 sq km (125,000 sq ml)
Population:	4,242,000
Capital:	Oslo (643,000)
Other cities:	Bergen (211,000) Trondheim (157,000)
Main primary products:	cereals, fish, oil, timber, gas, copper, iron, lead
Main industries:	Mining, oil refining, shipbuilding, food processing, fishing, forestry
Main exports:	Crude petroleum, metal products, natural gas, foodstuffs
Annual income per person:	$23,120
Infant mortality:	6 per 1,000 live births
Life expectancy (years):	Female 81, male 74
Adult literacy:	99 %

Figure B   Norway fact file

Figure C   Norway consumes 22 % of the HEP generated in Europe

HEP – energy for ever?

The development of Norway's HEP industry began in the early twentieth century, with the harnessing of energy from waterfalls flowing down the steep slopes above the coastal **fjords**. Later, inland sites were developed, the greatest concentration being in the Rjukan Valley 160 kilometres west of Oslo. As Figure D shows, Norway is Europe's biggest HEP consumer, with more than 99 % of its electricity coming from water power.

Hydro-electric power is a **renewable** form of energy, unlike fossil fuels. HEP is one of the world's main **sustainable** sources of energy. It has become a more attractive option as the world's supplies of coal, oil and gas have declined. It is also seen by many people as providing a solution to one of the major problems of fossil fuels, that of pollution.

In Norway, HEP has become a major source of power because of high levels of precipitation (1,500 millimetres per year on average), and the natural fall of water leaving mountainous areas in rivers. The distance water falls downwards is called the head. As much of Norway's precipitation falls high above sea level, there is great potential for the generation of electricity.

Country	HEP consumption million tonnes oil equivalent	% of world share
Austria	3.3	1.6
Finland	1.0	0.5
France	6.9	3.4
Germany	1.6	0.8
Italy	4.1	2.0
Norway	9.8	4.9
Sweden	5.1	2.5
Switzerland	3.2	1.6
Turkey	3.0	1.5
United Kingdom	0.6	0.3

Figure D   HEP consumption in Europe

HEP may be a sustainable form of energy, but is it really as environmentally friendly as has been suggested?

Arguments for:

- HEP provides cheap electricity, although the schemes are expensive to build. This encourages industrial growth, which is good for the Norwegian economy.
- HEP is a pollution-free energy source using natural renewable resources.
- HEP schemes open up some of the most remote areas of Norway. New roads are built when power stations are constructed.

Arguments against:

- Reservoirs built in the mountains for HEP schemes change the microclimate. This affects local animal and plant life.
- Rivers are a natural routeway, which are destroyed by the construction of dams.

Fossil fuels – boom then gloom?

Oil and gas were discovered in the North Sea in the 1960s. Since then, Norwegian as well as foreign oil companies have spent huge sums of money on prospecting, drilling and transporting oil and gas. Production has risen steadily, and Norway is now the world's seventh largest oil producer (see Figure E). Oil and gas together now make up over 50 % of the country's export earnings.

The government has spent much of the money from oil and gas locally, and the industries employ 70 % of the workforce locally. This has reduced unemployment problems caused by a decline in farming. Shipbuilding, another industry in decline, gained through the construction of modules for oil rigs. Oil and gas have stimulated the development of new technology which has benefited many other industries as well.

But oil is not a renewable resource, and production is expected to peak in the year 2000 at about 177 million tonnes. Norwegian gas is expected to have 65 years of production remaining. Heavily dependent on these industries, the Norwegian economy is affected by their highs and lows, particularly changes in the price of oil and gas.

Norway's greatest source of wealth is also its biggest environmental issue. Oil rigs and terminal buildings have transformed sparsely populated coastal areas. Safety zones around mainland buildings indicate the constant fear of accidents, and some farmland is lost. The monitoring and control of pollution is expensive. Huge anchor chains on oil platforms prevent fishing boats from putting down their nets, reducing catches. As with HEP, the development of Norway's fossil fuels has brought environmental costs as well as economic benefits.

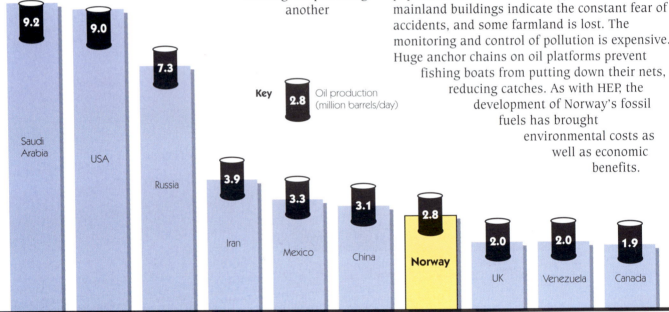

Key

2.8 Oil production (million barrels/day)

- Saudi Arabia 9.2
- USA 9.0
- Russia 7.3
- Iran 3.9
- Mexico 3.3
- China 3.1
- Norway 2.8
- UK 2.0
- Venezuela 2.0
- Canada 1.9

Figure E   The world's leading oil producers

Figure F   Oil in Norway – cost or benefit?

Figure G Energy and development – gain or loss?

Speech bubbles in Figure G:

- HEP is good for Norway. It's clean and safe.
- Cheap electricity from water power has brought lots of new industry into remote areas of the country.
- The HEP dams and reservoirs have ruined the look of the countryside. Who wants to come and look at a dam?
- Unemployment here is less than half the national average. Being near an oil terminal creates jobs for the local community.
- We depend almost totally on oil now. Many traditional jobs and skills are disappearing.
- Money from the oil and gas industries has kept our local hospital open. Who cares if the rigs and terminals are ugly?
- A river is natural – a dam is not. River transport and wildlife are ruined.
- The transport of oil and gas is supposed to be safe – but who knows?

▼ Questions

1 The energy revolution in Norway has affected the whole country. Figure G shows the opinions of some Norwegians. In addition to economic and environmental effects, the values and attitudes of people are important.

On a copy of the table opposite, write out each of the opinions in Figure G (above). Write a comment about each opinion, and tick the 'gain/loss' box where appropriate.

Statement	Comment	Environment	Economy
HEP is good for Norway. It's clean and safe.	_____	❏ gain / ❏ loss	❏ gain / ❏ loss
_____	_____	❏ gain / ❏ loss	❏ gain / ❏ loss
_____	_____	❏ gain / ❏ loss	❏ gain / ❏ loss

2 Which viewpoints do you think are the most important? Give reasons for your answer.
3 Hydro-electric power is called a sustainable form of energy. What does this mean?
4 Where in Britain do you think is most suitable for the development of HEP?
5 Research one form of sustainable energy other than HEP. How important is your chosen energy resource on a world-wide scale? How important could it be in the future? ➡

Review

Norway has rich energy resources in the form of oil, gas and hydro-electric power. The harnessing of these resources has transformed Norway into one of the richest countries in Europe. Each resource brings economic gains, as well as environmental problems. The future of energy use in Norway must balance these costs and benefits.

Managing the coastline

Key ideas & questions

- Natural changes and human activities may create problems for people who live and work in coastal areas.
- The Netherlands manages the threat of coastal flooding with a system of barriers and other methods.
- Extensive management of the coastline has enabled Rotterdam – Europoort to grow into the world's largest port.

Main activity

Assessing the costs and benefits of coastal management in the Netherlands. Outlining the development of Europoort by means of a sketch map and case study card.

Figure A   The Netherlands – nearly a quarter of the land surface is below sea level

CASE STUDY: The Netherlands coastline

The struggle against the sea

Do you know?

? Much of the western part of the Netherlands is below sea level.

? The country is highly urbanised, and is one of the most densely populated countries in the world.

? Industrial and population growth has led to transport congestion. There are 84 times as many cars in the Netherlands as there were in 1947.

The Netherlands is a flat, low-lying country criss-crossed by waterways, in which settlement was only really possible once **dikes** had been built to withstand the sea. The country has always taken advantage of its position on the sea and, as a result, the low-lying western coastal areas have become the most densely populated. In the Netherlands 60 % of the population live in the 24 % of the country that is below sea level (see Figure A).

About two thirds of the country would regularly be flooded without protection. Flooding affects land above sea level as well as below, also affecting much of the land near to rivers. The Netherlands is really a large **delta**, where the Rhine and Maas rivers reach the North Sea. The country lives in fear of both coastal and river flooding.

Figure B   Bulb fields – a polder landscape

Polders

A **polder** is an area of reclaimed land which is mainly surrounded by raised banks called dikes, within which water levels can be controlled. Some polders are as much as seven metres below sea level. More water generally enters a polder than can be used or drained naturally. The water has to be pumped into the nearest river or sea.

Almost the entire west and low north of the Netherlands (50 % of the total land area) consists of polders. The Zuider Zee in the north of the country was closed off in 1932, creating the fresh water Ijsselmeer. Since then,

four of the five polders originally planned have been completed.

Most of the land reclaimed by polders is used for farming. Figure B, is typical. The actual land use is determined more often by how well the water level is controlled rather than the quality of the soil. Polder land is often very fertile and sought after. In Flevoland, for example, yields of potatoes, sugar beet and wheat are among the highest in the country, with market gardening also being important.

Figure C The Zuider Zee Scheme

The Zuider Zee scheme

The Zuider Zee was closed off from the sea by a 30 kilometre barrier dam, completed in 1932. The freshwater lake created behind the dam became known as the Ijsselmeer (see Figure C). Food shortages during the First World War, and severe flooding in 1916, had convinced the government of the need to take action. By 1968, four polders had been drained. The combined area of these polders is 1,650 square kilometres, 5 % of the total area of the Netherlands.

The draining of the polders gave the government the chance to create a planned environment. In the original plans, the polders were to be used to increase agricultural output. Farms and roads were designed in a grid pattern. After the Second World War, however, there was a change in land-use planning. To cope with a growing population, parts of the polders were used for housing. The new towns of Lamer and Leylstadt, for example, act as overspill towns for Amsterdam. Elsewhere, industrial estates have been built, and areas set aside for leisure activities.

The government originally planned to drain five polders (see Figure C). The fifth, the Markerwaard, was to be made by draining water from Marken Lake. In 1991, after more than 20 years of debate, the government decided to abandon plans to reclaim this polder. A decline in population growth was one of the factors contributing to this decision.

The reclamation has greatly reduced the risk of flooding in the 'old' land around the Ijsselmeer. Another benefit is that travelling times between areas near the Ijsselmeer have been cut by new roads, including one along the barrier dam itself. However, not all the effects have been good. The natural environment has been altered by the creation of an artificial lake, as well as new land. Some villages on the shores of the Zuider Zee made their living from fishing, which is now impossible.

The Delta Project

The south-west of the Netherlands consists of a series of islands between which the Rhine, Maas and Scheldt rivers find their way to the sea (see Figure D). Much land has been reclaimed from the sea, and the whole area is at risk from the floods that repeatedly threaten this part of the country.

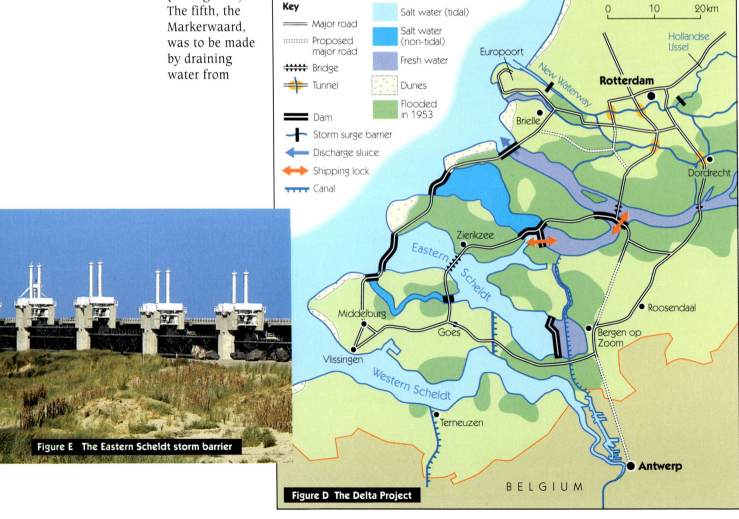

Figure E   The Eastern Scheldt storm barrier

Figure D The Delta Project

Key
- ══ Major road
- ⋯⋯ Proposed major road
- ⋙ Bridge
- ⊕ Tunnel
- ▬ Dam
- ╪ Storm surge barrier
- ◀ Discharge sluice
- ⬌ Shipping lock
- ⬚ Canal

- Salt water (tidal)
- Salt water (non-tidal)
- Fresh water
- Dunes
- Flooded in 1953

Europoort · New Waterway · Rotterdam · Hollandse Ijssel · Brielle · Dordrecht · Zierikzee · Eastern Scheldt · Middelburg · Goes · Roosendaal · Bergen op Zoom · Vlissingen · Western Scheldt · Terneuzen · Antwerp · BELGIUM

0   10   20km

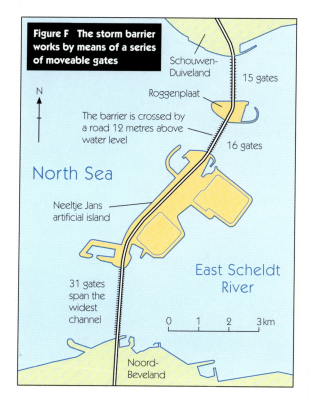

Figure F The storm barrier works by means of a series of moveable gates

Schouwen-Duiveland

15 gates

Roggenplaat

The barrier is crossed by a road 12 metres above water level

16 gates

North Sea

Neeltje Jans artificial island

31 gates span the widest channel

East Scheldt River

0 1 2 3km

Noord-Beveland

The 1953 floods

As early as 1950, a dam had been built along the stretch of coastline near Rotterdam. The devastating floods of 1953 led to a co-ordinated plan to be put into action.

On 1 February, 200,000 hectares of south-west Netherlands were flooded, killing more than 1,800 people. The disaster occurred because of a combination of circumstances. A deep depression, with hurricane force winds, lashed the Dutch coast. This coincided with very high spring tide levels. As well as these natural causes, the upkeep of dikes had been neglected during and after the Second World War.

In the 30 years following the 1953 floods, nine dams were built to protect the low-lying land from the sea (see Figure D). The protection of reclaimed land was more important than trying to reclaim any more land from the sea.

The Delta project has had an enormous impact on the area. The main aim of the scheme has been achieved, in that there is now much less danger of flooding. Roads over the dams and bridges linking them have improved the accessibility of what were once isolated islands; the coastline has been reduced from 800 to 80 kilometres.

The Eastern Scheldt – Storm Barrier

The largest part of the Delta project is the eight kilometre long storm surge barrier on the Eastern Scheldt river (see Figure E).

The original plan was to close off the mouth of the river completely, creating a freshwater

lake behind a dam. This plan met with strong opposition among many people, who felt that the environment, and wildlife in particular, would be affected. They argued that the land could be protected just as well by raising and reinforcing the banks of the river. Local farmers, however, wanted the creation of a freshwater lake. This would stop salt water seeping into their newly created polders, which ruined many crops. More polders could then be drained when there was demand for more land.

A compromise was eventually reached, which was to have an opening barrier, (see Figure F). Massive concrete piles were sunk into the river, supporting a total of 62 moveable gates. The 45 metre wide gates are only lowered when there is a high flood risk, which, on average, happens once or twice a year. Usually the gates are kept in the raised position.

	Environmental Costs / Benefits	Economic Costs / Benefits
Zuider Zee Scheme	Changing natural environment	Loss of fishing villages
Delta Project	_____	_____

Figure G Assessing the costs and benefits of the Delta Project

▼ Questions

1 Why was the Zuider Zee scheme started?
2 What was the main aim of the Delta project?
3 Draw sketch maps to show the main features of the Zuider Zee and Delta projects. For each map, you should use annotations (or labels) to describe the features.
4 Why do you think there is no dam across the Western Scheldt river?
5 Why did the government decide not to drain the fifth polder in the Zuider Zee scheme?
6 What effects might the barrier have upon the environment and wildlife of the area?
7 Why do you think an opening barrier was built rather than a dam?
8 The barrier is dotted with windmills. What are these windmills for? Why is the barrier a good location for windmills?
9 In order to summarise the costs and benefits of the Dutch coastal protection schemes, make a copy of Figure G. In each box, write relevant comments. One has been completed to help you.
10 Do you think the benefits of each scheme are greater than the costs? Give reasons for your answer.
11 Who do you think should pay for protecting the coastline? Why?
12 'We should do nothing. It is too costly, and not certain to prevent flooding anyway. It is better to pay for the cost of flooding when it happens.' What do you think of this viewpoint?
13 The Camargue area of southern France is another coastal area requiring careful management (see pages 33–37). What similarities and differences are there in the ways in which the two areas are managed?

Figure H Rotterdam – Europoort

Figure I Rotterdam in 1947

Figure K Rotterdam – Europoort in 1980

Figure J The island of Rosenburg (1) and the Hoek van Holland (2)

Rotterdam – Europoort

Management of the Dutch coastline has changed both the size and the shape of the country. The Delta Project has reduced the length of coastline by over 700 kilometres, and has dramatically changed the character of the region. The development of ports has seen some of the most spectacular changes, particularly the growth of **Rotterdam** and the **Europoort** complex (see Figure H).

Rotterdam began to grow as a port in the nineteenth century with the opening of a direct link between the city and the North Sea. The New Waterway gave access to the sea from centres of industrialisation like the Ruhr in Germany.

An atlas map of the area in 1947 (Figure I), clearly shows the route of the New Waterway. The aerial photograph (Figure J) shows the Waterway cutting between the **Hoek van Holland (2), and the Beer of Hoek van Holland (1)**, which is the edge of the island of Rosenburg.

The post-war years have seen the growth of Rotterdam into the world's leading port. The 1980 map in Figure K shows how the area had been transformed in little over 30 years.

The port became an important centre for the handling and distribution of container goods. Large containers of standard size can be packed with freight, and transferred from one mode of transport to another quickly and cheaply. The Eemhaven complex, marked 'A' on Figure K, is home to European Combined Terminals, the world's largest container handling company. As well as waterways, Rotterdam is served by rapid road and rail networks. These transport networks enable the city to serve a catchment area, or hinterland, which extends as far as Belgium and Germany.

In the 1960s and 1970s, the port expanded rapidly to the west of the city of Rotterdam, forming the Europoort complex. Over half of the island of Rosenburg was dug out to make way for new docks and shipping routes. In the decade after excavation started in 1958, the growth of Europoort continued along the southern bank of the New Waterway towards the sea. With no reduction in industrial expansion being apparent, the Dutch government decided to extend the port westwards into the sea. The reclaimed Maasvlakte ('B' on Figure K) completed a 25 kilometre stretch of docks and industrial sites to the west of Rotterdam.

The dredging of deep harbour basins has made Europoort accessible to the world's largest tankers. As a result of this, and the tendency to locate refineries close to the market for oil, Europoort has become Europe's main centre of the petrochemicals industry. Five large oil refineries have located here, for example on Maasvlakte. A comparison of the map (Figure M) with the earlier aerial photograph of the same area indicates dramatically the extent to which the coastline has been altered.

Figure L Europoort serves some of the world's largest container companies

Rotterdam – Europoort is one of the world's leading industrial complexes. It has done much to enhance the position of the Netherlands as an important distribution centre for Europe, yet its development has not been without problems. Industries such as food processing, brewing and petrochemicals have polluted the environment as well as bringing increased prosperity. Transport links through the Netherlands may provide quick access to the port, but Europoort itself is well known for its congestion problems. These could become worse if the Dutch government decide to extend Europoort further out into the North Sea.

▼ Questions

14 Draw a labelled sketch map from the 1:50,000 map (Figure M) to show the following
- Hoek van Holland
- Maasvlakte
- ECT – container terminal
- The main oil terminal areas (red circles)
- Shade in the approximate area of the island of Rosenburg that has been removed.

15 Use the information on Europoort to compile a case study card. This should contain a summary of the main points you need to know on a card sized 20 cm by 13 cm (the size of a postcard). Case study cards are useful when revising any topic.

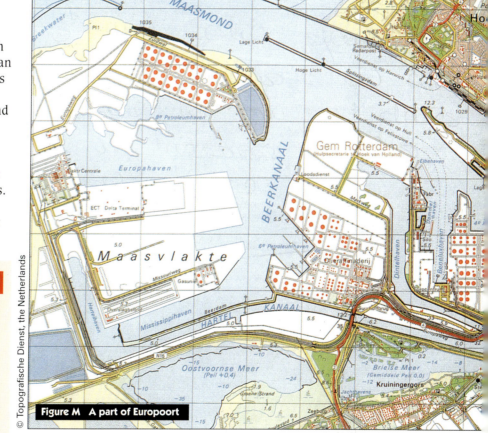

© Topografische Dienst, the Netherlands

Figure M A part of Europoort

Review

The Zuider Zee and Delta projects have both brought great benefits to the people of the Netherlands. The risk of flooding has been greatly reduced, and new land made available. There have also been costs and problems with each scheme. The dams and dikes are expensive to build and maintain, and affect the environment. There is doubt as to whether even the strongest dikes would be able to prevent the type of flooding which caused such devastation in 1953. One of the greatest changes to the coastline has been the development of Europoort, the world's leading port.

Tourism and the environment

Key ideas & questions

- Why is tourism so important in southern Spain?
- What benefits has tourism brought to Spain?
- What are the problems caused by tourism, and how do people respond to them?
- What are the pressures facing the **Camargue** in southern France? How could these problems be managed?

Main activity

A problem-solving exercise based on proposals for the future of the Camargue Nature Park in France, together with questions relating to the Spanish tourist industry.

Tourism has developed as a major industry and source of employment in the second half of the twentieth century. Improvements in transport, greater affluence, and higher expectations have resulted in an increasing number of people taking holidays in Europe. The tourist industry makes a significant contribution to the economy of many European countries. France receives the most from tourists, over $25 billion per year, attracting over 50 million visitors (see Figure A). The 'multiplier effect' of tourism is enormous. The industry creates employment not just in accommodation and catering, but also in activities such as banking, entertainments, and crafts. Within the European Union, 7 % of the workforce are employed in jobs related to tourism, generating 5.5 % of the EU's wealth.

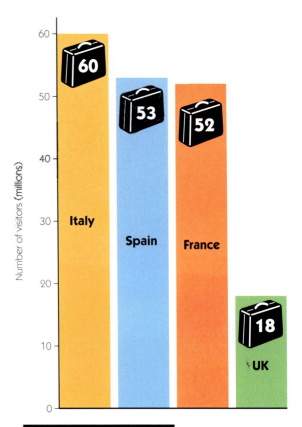

Figure A   Tourist destinations

Figure B   Natural and historical attractions make France a popular tourist destination

Do you know?

❓ The river Rhône is 750 km in length.
❓ On the last section of its journey to the Mediterranean Sea, the Rhône valley separates the Massif Central from the French Alps.
❓ Five nuclear power plants are located on the banks of the Rhône, which is also an important source of hydro-electric power.

France is a popular destination for tourists from throughout Europe and further afield.

The country provides a wealth of natural and cultural attractions (see Figure B), and with government assistance tourism is one of France's main growth industries. The French government has established National and Regional Parks in order to cope with pressures caused by the increasing number of visitors both from home and abroad (see Figure C). These are areas where the natural environment needs to be protected from unlimited access. One such area is the Camargue Regional Park at the mouth of the river Rhône in southern France.

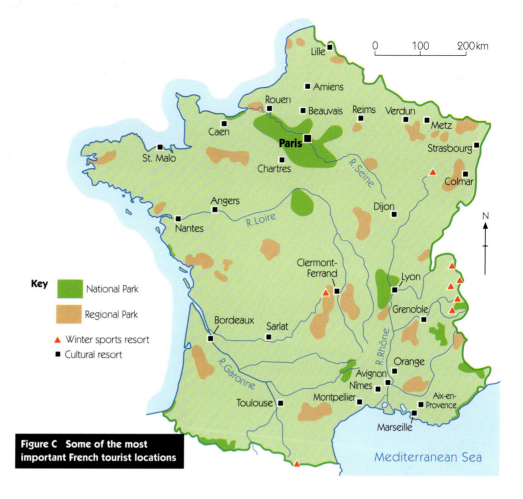

Key
- National Park
- Regional Park
- ▲ Winter sports resort
- ■ Cultural resort

Figure C Some of the most important French tourist locations

CASE STUDY: The Camargue

The river Rhône is one of the longest rivers in France. Canals link the river with locations as distant as Paris and the river Rhine, making the Rhône a major inland waterway. The river eventually flows into the Mediterranean Sea, forming a large delta of lakes, marshes and river channels (see Figure D).

This delta, called the Camargue, covers over 500 square kilometres. Of this, 40 % is used for farmland, notably irrigated areas for rice cultivation. The mild wet winters are ideal for grass growth, and sheep are moved down from higher mountain pastures for the winter.

However, the Camargue is most famous for the wildlife which has inhabited the region longer than its people (see Figure E). The marshes attract birds on their migration routes to and from Africa. Others, like the pink flamingos, live permanently in the delta. Wild horses and black bulls roam the remote parts of the Camargue where there is little sign of human impact.

The area surrounding the Etang de Vaccarès forms the Camargue Nature Park (see Figure F). This biological and zoological reserve of 15,000 hectares restricts public access in order to conserve the environment. This has been a success, but the Camargue faces increased pressure from people who want to use the land.

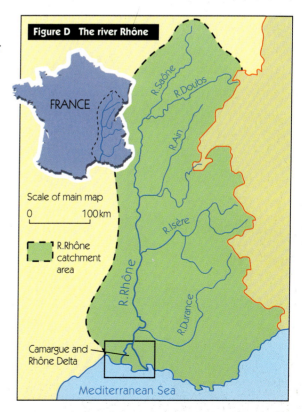

Figure D The river Rhône

FRANCE

Scale of main map
0   100km

R.Rhône catchment area

Camargue and Rhône Delta

Mediterranean Sea

Figure E Wildlife of the Camargue

Figure F The Camargue

Pressures on the Camargue

The growth of agriculture, industry and tourism is vital for the economic prosperity of the region. Yet all make demands upon the limited resources of this fragile environment, and they are sometimes in direct conflict with each other. Wetlands are under threat from demands for increased rice production, while some marshes have been drained to provide grazing land for sheep. It is the development of industry and tourism which pose the greatest problems for the future of the Camargue.

The long hot summers, with temperatures up to 35 °C, evaporate much of the marsh waters, leaving salt pans. Although salt farms are an important part of the landscape, it is industrial pollution from Mediterranean ports which is the greatest threat to the natural environment. Marseilles, to the east, is the largest port in France. The industrial complex of Fos lies on the eastern edge of the delta. Until recently, Fos-sur-Mer was a tiny **hamlet** overlooking marshy flats. Today it is a centre for steel and petrochemical works, its development funded partly by the French government and partly by private industry.

The Mediterranean is virtually tideless, and almost landlocked. As a result, pollution which enters the sea cannot easily escape; the Mediterranean and its surrounding shores are among the most polluted in the world (see Figure G). The Rhône and other rivers which flow into the sea contain waste from factories, and fertilisers and pesticides that have been washed off farmland. The Rhône contributes to the 1.5 million tonnes of chemicals dumped into the Mediterranean each year. Much of this pollution stays close to the shore in the calm, sheltered waters.

Every year, more than 200 million visitors holiday in the area, making the Mediterranean the most popular tourist destination in the world. This places great strain on the natural environment. Holidaymakers use far more of the precious resources like water than local residents. They also create an enormous amount of waste, most of which is pumped untreated into the sea. In some areas tourists 'camp' on the beaches which adds to the environmental problems.

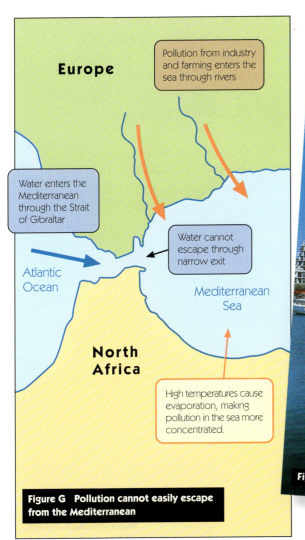

Figure G Pollution cannot easily escape from the Mediterranean

Europe

Pollution from industry and farming enters the sea through rivers

Water enters the Mediterranean through the Strait of Gibraltar

Water cannot escape through narrow exit

Atlantic Ocean

Mediterranean Sea

North Africa

High temperatures cause evaporation, making pollution in the sea more concentrated.

Figure H La Grande Motte

The French government has been eager to develop tourism in the area. Since the 1960s, it has funded the building of 'New World' towns along the Mediterranean coast, specialising in tourist accommodation. The largest of these towns is La Grande Motte (see Figure H). The resort is built along a four kilometre beach, has facilities for mooring 2,000 craft, and campsites capable of accommodating 15,000 people. La Grande Motte is perhaps best known for its many pyramid shaped apartment buildings (see Figure I). The New World towns are crowded in summer, although they offer little in the way of employment for local residents out of the holiday season. Tourist development has already taken place in the Nature Park, at Saintes-Maries-de-la-Mer. Further expansion is likely to be at the expense of the Camargue as a relatively unspoilt wilderness.

The most audacious and distinctive of the 'New World' towns, La Grande Motte rises like a science fiction city at the western end of the Camargue. Its white stepped pyramids containing thousands of apartments were formulated by architects and engineers in the 1960s.

The pyramids and still less orthodox buildings are conspicuous from near and far. For some, while clean and fashionable, La Grande Motte lacks the substance given by a longer period of history. The new resorts along this coastline have stretched to the very edge of the delta. Port Camargue has been created from former marshland. Because the development is low rise, there is little to interrupt the vast, watery spaciousness characteristic of the Camargue itself.

Figure I   A visitor's view of La Grande Motte

Dear Student,

Welcome! I hope that you enjoy your time with us in France. As you know, the Camargue is one of France's Regional Parks, and as such it enjoys a degree of protection from visitors and from future development.

Since the 1960s, tourist facilities have spread along our stretch of coastline. The delta of the river Rhône, the Camargue, remains one area with relatively few visitors. Tourism is a major contributor to the local and French economies, and as such the national government has encouraged the growth of tourism where possible. Many resorts have grown with the help of government money.

The Camargue now faces many pressures. In addition to agriculture and industry, it is expected that applications will soon arrive regarding developments within the delta, affecting the Regional Park itself. We would be grateful for your considered opinion regarding the future of the Park. Should development be encouraged, should we encourage a 'soft tourism' approach, or does the Camargue need to be preserved at all costs?

We look forward to receiving your report in the near future.

Yours sincerely,

M Carter

Figure J   Your task...

More tourists means more money. People camping and staying in apartments will need to buy food and drinks from my supermarket. I'm in favour of encouraging tourists to the area.

Local shopkeeper

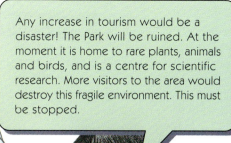

Any increase in tourism would be a disaster! The Park will be ruined. At the moment it is home to rare plants, animals and birds, and is a centre for scientific research. More visitors to the area would destroy this fragile environment. This must be stopped.

There is more demand for fresh water than the region can supply. The tourist industry is a major user of water. We will have to look at expensive schemes to transfer water from other regions if more tourist developments are built.

Engineer

Conservationist

We would like to see more hotels and other tourist facilities in the area. There are many natural and cultural attractions, and we believe many more people would visit if there were more facilities.

I can see the problems; more visitors, more cars on narrow roads, crowding and pollution. But tourism is big business, and encouraging more people to visit would help the local economy and create jobs in an area of high unemployment.

Sunshine Holidays travel representative

Local resident

Figure K   Some opinions

Solutions

1 Tourism should be encouraged, and the Nature Park opened up to the public. Access roads should be built into the Park, draining marshland where necessary. Government funding could be used to develop tourist centres around the Camargue. This proposal would make a significant contribution to the economy of the south of France.

2 A 'soft tourism' approach should be adopted. This is where the tourist industry takes second place to other activities, and no special facilities are provided for tourists. Tourism is important to the local economy, but building more facilities and encouraging visitors would damage the natural environment.

3 The Camargue Nature Park should be preserved. It is one of the few wilderness areas remaining in Europe, and as such it is of international importance. The French government should give financial assistance to the area. If local people have good jobs in farming or industry, they will not need to rely on tourism. Visitors should be actively encouraged to go elsewhere; there are other areas in France where the environment is not so fragile.

Figure L   Solutions

▼ Questions

For the purpose of this activity, imagine that you are a student studying for a course in town and country planning. Part of your course involves spending time in the south of France. You have been asked to prepare a report about the future of the Camargue (see Figures J–L).

Use all the resources on pages 32–37 in order to write your report, which should include the following sections:

1 A summary of the problems facing the Camargue.

2 An outline of the proposed solutions.

3 An evaluation of the solutions. What are the good and bad points about each of them? Which proposal do you favour?

4 A plan for how your chosen solution could be made to work. Your suggestions should be realistic, and could be supported by sketch maps and diagrams.

Figure A   The location of Spain's main beaches and coastal resorts

Key
- Major resort
- Sandy beach

France

Lloret de Mar
Costa Brava

Costa Dorada

SPAIN

Portugal

Minorca

Palma

Majorca

Ibiza

Balearic Islands

Costa del Azahar

Benidorm

Costa Blanca

Canaries resorts:
1 Playa de las Américas
2 Playa del Inglés
3 Betancuria
4 Arrecife

Torremolinos

Marbella

Costa de la Luz

Costa del Sol

Costa del Almeria

Lanzarote

Canary Islands

Tenerife

Africa

Spain is one of the most popular tourist destinations in the world. It is visited annually by over 80 million holidaymakers. Most of these visitors stay at the coast, in resorts on the Spanish mainland or the Balearic and Canary Islands. Tourism has grown to be the most important industry in Spain. It employs 11 % of the Spanish workforce, and contributes 20 % to the country's wealth.

Tourism is an important industry to many regions of Spain, and the Spanish government has recently attempted to attract visitors to some of the less well known parts of the country. Despite this, Spain is most famous for its coastal resorts (see Figure A), where 80 % of tourists stay. The most popular locations are the Canary and Balearic Islands, which attract 60 % of all visitors to the country. The largest number of visitors is from the United Kingdom, followed by Germany, France, the Netherlands and Belgium. The Mediterranean coastline contains a chain of resorts, from the Costa Brava, north of Barcelona, to the Costa del Sol in the south. In the 1950s there were relatively few large

Figure B   The combination of sea, sun and open beaches, together with spectacular inland scenery, made southern Spain ideal for the growth of mass tourism

Figure C   Villages in the Sierra Bermeja hills provided workers for the coastal resorts

resorts in Spain. The growth of tourism on the Mediterranean coast in the last 40 years has been remarkable, and has been due to a combination of factors:

1 Located in the south of Europe, the climate of Spain is one of the warmest in the continent. The Costa del Sol receives 3,000 hours of sunshine per year, with average July temperatures of 27 °C (compared to 17 °C for London). The southern coast of Spain is also one of the driest in Europe, notably the area around Almeria. Summer droughts may cause problems for farmers, but they are exactly what most tourists like. The Mediterranean climate in the winter is cooler and wetter, but still compares favourably with most of Europe, particularly the north. The almost guaranteed good summer weather and pleasant winter conditions ensure that the Spanish Mediterranean is popular all year round.

2 The environment is ideal for the development of a coastal tourist industry. The Mediterranean Sea is virtually tideless, and is warm all year round. Much of the coastline is fringed by sandy beaches. The mountainous scenery inland provides a dramatic contrast for tourists who wander from the beaches.

3 The growth of the 'package holiday' in the late 1950s and early 1960s. Spain and Italy were the first destinations for these holidays, where tourists bought an 'all in package', including flight, accommodation and meals. By block booking hotel accommodation, travel agents and tour companies were able to offer holidays at relatively cheap prices, in good quality hotels. Local tour representatives were generally present to deal with problems, and to organise entertainments. Hotel complexes sprang up all along the Mediterranean coast.

4 The southern Spanish region of Andalusia is the poorest in the country. The growing tourist industry was able to recruit local labour, particularly from small inland farming villages (see Figure C), paying low wages. Tourism gave a major boost to the economy of southern Spain. The Spanish government encouraged this growth by providing funds from the national government, together with money from the European Union (see pages 63–70).

5 The airport at Malaga and good coastal roads meant that resorts were easily accessible. Tourists could arrive at their destinations quickly, even though many inland areas remained inaccessible.

Torremolinos – capital of the Costa del Sol

Figure D   Torremolinos

Figure E   The village of Torremolinos

Torremolinos illustrates both the effects of tourism on the local area, and changes in the tourist industry in Spain. The self-proclaimed capital of the south coast of Spain lies to the south-west of the city of Malaga (see Figure D). In the 1950s, Torremolinos was a small village with no holiday developments (Figure E). Its beaches, climate and location near to Malaga ensured that Torremolinos was in the forefront of tourist development in the area. Flights to Malaga airport meant that the resort could be reached easily and quickly. The area became so popular that a new terminal needed to be built at the airport. As the beach front became crowded, high rise hotel complexes were built to make the best use of limited space (see Figure F). Luxury hotels catered for the waves of British and German visitors. The holiday industry provided employment for locals and for many who migrated to the area from surrounding villages.

The tourist industry of Torremolinos and the Costas is changing. Many of the luxury hotels which were once full all summer now stand half empty. Spain has become relatively expensive as a tourist destination. Consumers are provided with an increasing range of holiday locations, many of which now provide better value than Spain. Long haul holidays to places such as Africa and the Caribbean provide attractive alternatives.

Torremolinos has struggled to move away from its downmarket image. The crowded sea front, rows of discos, and shops providing a 'home from home' atmosphere has become less popular with British and German tourists, who make up the majority of visitors. The crowded resort is unable to cater for the growth in popularity of activity based holidays.

Self-catering accommodation has grown in popularity in the resort. People are spending less in the large and luxury hotels. As a result, many local workers are on temporary contracts, dependent upon the flow of visitors. The tourist industry, as well as not paying high wages, does not offer job security.

The Spanish government has encouraged the diversification of tourism in the country. Cities like Seville, the capital of Andalusia, offer cultural and historical attractions not available on the Costas. In the long term, while the number of visitors to Spain may not decrease, the relative importance of the Mediterranean resorts is likely to decline.

Figure F Bajondillo beach, Torremolinos

Figure G   The location of Seville

River Guadalquivir

Coto de Donana

SEVILLE

N

Almeria

Malaga

0   100 km

Atlantic Ocean

Mediterranean Sea

Strait of Gibraltar

MOROCCO

Ceuta

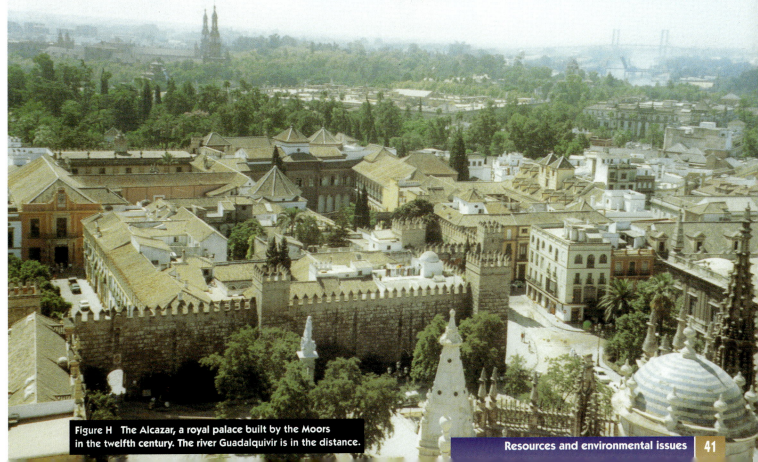

Figure H   The Alcazar, a royal palace built by the Moors in the twelfth century. The river Guadalquivir is in the distance.

Seville is the largest city in Andalusia with a population of nearly 700,000, making it the fourth largest city in Spain. Located near the mouth of the river Guadalquivir (Figure G), Seville has long been an important port and commercial centre for the region. In the fifteenth and sixteenth centuries the city was the only port authorised to trade with Spain's American colonies, making it the most important city in the country. The city has a growing tourist industry based on its cultural and historical attractions, particularly its architecture. Many of Seville's buildings date from the Middle Ages. The most famous of these are the Alcazar (see Figure H), a royal palace built in the twelfth century by the north African Moors who ruled the city for five centuries, and a vast sixteenth-century cathedral. The Spanish government has tried to encourage the growth of tourism in Seville, although many visitors are day trippers from the coastal resorts. The World Fair 'EXPO '92' was held in Seville, leading to improvements in transport and communication in the area.

Figure I Satellite image of the Strait of Gibraltar, showing the Spanish coastline as far east as Torremolinos, and part of Morocco

▼ Questions

Use Figure D to answer the following questions:

1 What is the most southerly point of the Spanish mainland?
2 What is the name of the road linking the towns on the coast?
3 Why do you think there is little development inland of the main road?
4 What are the main effects of tourism on Andalusia. Summarise your answer under the headings a) costs and b) benefits.
5 Look at the satellite image (Figure I), showing part of the Spanish mainland and north Africa. Draw a sketch of the photograph, and use Figure D to label the following on to your sketch:

a) The Strait of Gibraltar   b) Gibraltar   c) Tarifa
d) Algiceras   e) Torremolinos   f) Marbella
g) La Linea   h) The main coastal road   i) The Mediterranean Sea
j) Highland

Use an atlas to add:
k) Morocco   l) Tangiers   m) Cueta (Spanish territory).

Review

Tourism has become an important industry in the second half of the twentieth century. France offers many attractions for the tourist, and the French government has been keen to encourage the growth of the industry. Some natural environments are sensitive, and the development of tourism needs careful management. One such area is the Camargue in France, at the mouth of the river Rhône.

Spain is one of the world's most popular tourist destinations. The growth in package holidays, together with the Mediterranean Sea and climate, have led to a tourist boom in southern Spain. This sudden growth has brought problems as well as benefits to Spain.

The North Sea – an international issue

Key ideas & questions

● Why is the North Sea an important resource?
● What are the effects of people's use of the North Sea?
● How can the use of the North Sea best be developed and managed?

Main activity

A simulation concerning the future management of the North Sea, together with background questions.

CASE STUDY: Fishing and the oil industry

Figure A   The North Sea

The North Sea is bordered by eight countries (see Figure A) which have used it as a resource and a waste dump for centuries. Until recently it was wrongly assumed that the sea was large enough to cope. As an international sea, its management is not the responsibility of any individual country. The problems of pollution and overfishing have turned a rich **ecosystem** into a potential environmental disaster.

The quantity and range of pollutants are bringing the North Sea to crisis point (see Figure B). Waste from the numerous industrial and urban areas surrounding the sea is the biggest problem; nearly half of the oil contaminating the North Sea comes from land based industries. Nutrients from fertilisers used in farming deprive the sea of oxygen, killing marine life.

Do you know?

? The North Sea is one of the most productive waters in the world.

? There are over 200 species of fish in the North Sea.

? Stocks of cod, herring, plaice and mackerel are currently being overfished and face possible extinction.

? European Union countries have increased the amount of money they give to help fishermen (**subsidies**). They build bigger boats, which catch more and more fish.

? The North Sea is also badly polluted. More than 1,000 new chemicals are manufactured each year, and nobody knows what happens to them when they enter the sea.

? There will shortly be over 400 unwanted oil and gas rigs in the North Sea.

? International conferences have failed to agree on what needs to be done to save the North Sea.

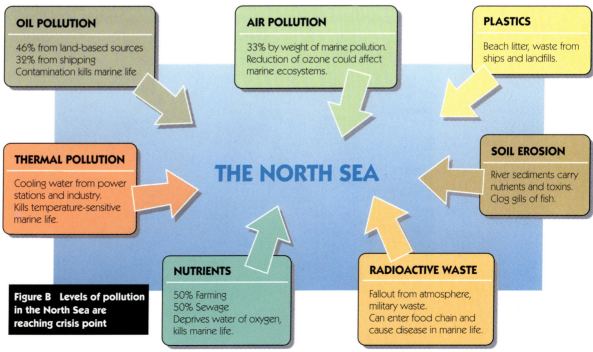

OIL POLLUTION

46% from land-based sources
32% from shipping
Contamination kills marine life

AIR POLLUTION

33% by weight of marine pollution. Reduction of ozone could affect marine ecosystems.

PLASTICS

Beach litter, waste from ships and landfills.

THERMAL POLLUTION

Cooling water from power stations and industry. Kills temperature-sensitive marine life.

SOIL EROSION

River sediments carry nutrients and toxins. Clog gills of fish.

THE NORTH SEA

NUTRIENTS

50% Farming
50% Sewage
Deprives water of oxygen, kills marine life.

RADIOACTIVE WASTE

Fallout from atmosphere, military waste. Can enter food chain and cause disease in marine life.

Figure B   Levels of pollution in the North Sea are reaching crisis point

Figure C From land or sea, oil pollution is difficult to remove

Are the chips down for North Sea fish?

The North Sea is one of the most productive fishing areas in the world. There are over 200 species of fish in the sea, of which 12 make up over 90 % of the catch landed by fishermen. Over-fishing has caused a spectacular collapse in the number of fish, such as herring and mackerel, which will be halted only with careful management and international agreement.

Herring stocks in the North Sea have supported fisheries for several centuries in Denmark, Sweden, Norway and the UK. They have made a significant contribution to the economic growth of these countries.

Herring shoals reach enormous proportions, sometimes containing several thousand tonnes of fish. These are easily located and caught using echo-sounding equipment. A peak of 1.7 million tonnes of herring were taken from the North Sea in 1966.

However, this amount of fishing could not be sustained. An increasing number of small fish, often only one year old, were being caught in huge nets along with fully grown herring, then processed into oil and fish meal. The numbers of herring could not recover, and by 1969 the catch had dropped to 24,000 tonnes. The mortality index (see Figure E) shows that something had to be done to preserve herring stocks for the future.

From 1970, regulations were introduced limiting the number of fish caught, stating a minimum size, and banning fish oil and meal production. European governments had to agree on the amount of fish caught by each country, called a *quota*. Stocks slowly recovered, but to only a fraction of what they had once been.

The total amount of herring that may be taken out of the North Sea is called the *Total Allowable Catch* (TAC). This was 440,000 tonnes in 1995, but was reduced to 230,000 tonnes in 1996 in a renewed effort to preserve stocks. The problem is made worse by some countries deciding upon their own quotas without agreement. In 1995, Iceland announced that it would take an additional 250,000 tonnes of herring from the North Sea. In addition, herring are fished by nations not included in these formal quotas.

Figure D Pressure groups such as Greenpeace campaign against the over-use of the North Sea. Here, activists protest against industrial fishing off the east coast of Scotland.

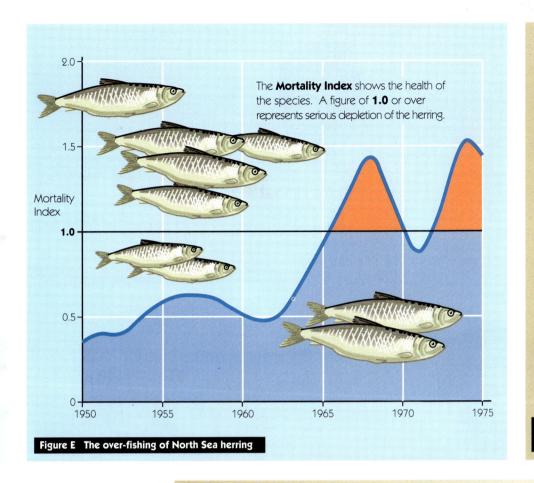

The **Mortality Index** shows the health of the species. A figure of **1.0** or over represents serious depletion of the herring.

Figure E   The over-fishing of North Sea herring

Participating countries:

Norway

Denmark

Belgium

United Kingdom

Sweden

Germany

France

The Netherlands

The following are present as observers:

Greenpeace

Friends of the Earth

The Oil Industry Production Group

The International Chamber
   of Shipping

Figure F   Participating countries and observers

Outline of topics for discussion at the North Sea conference

1   Protection of species and habitats:
Pollution and modern fishing methods are probably the most serious threats to marine wildlife. Habitats need to be protected from over-fishing.

2   Hazardous substances:
New substances are continually entering the sea. This problem needs to be reduced by eliminating waste inputs, and enforcing the 'polluter pays' principle.

3   Nutrients:
Main sources of nutrients include partly treated urban waste and modern agriculture, which lead to a reduction of oxygen in sea water. A target for the reduction of nutrients needs to be agreed if fish stocks are to be saved.

4   Fisheries:
The North Sea is being over-fished. Many stocks are seriously depleted, and some modern methods catch fish other than those required. The EU Common Fisheries Policy must have environmental as well as economic aims.

5   Pollution from ships:
Oil, chemicals and sewage from ships pollute the sea. The deliberate dumping of waste must be policed.

6   Discharge and disposal of Radioactive Substances:
Many activities in the nuclear industry pose a threat to the marine environment. The dumping of processed fuel is a major threat.

Figure G   The North Sea conference

It is important that a balance is struck between the needs of different groups of people, who may want different things from the North Sea. We recognise that fish stocks are limited, and that quotas have to be set. The amount of toxic material emptied into the sea must be reduced. However, fishing is an important industry, and we have a responsibility to protect the livelihood of our fishermen. Many countries ignore the quotas that are set. We also feel reluctant to pay heavily to clear up pollution for which we are not responsible.

Spokesperson for the United Kingdom Government

Friends of the Earth is concerned about over-fishing in the North Sea. The organisation believes that attempts at management in the past have not worked. To reduce over-fishing the European Union must offer fishermen an alternative method of earning their living. Strict quotas must be enforced, and EU governments must not turn a blind eye to those who ignore the law. Fewer fish must be caught, from a wider range of species, if the North Sea is to remain a resource for future generations.

Spokesperson for Friends of the Earth

At current production rates the world's oil reserves will only last for 43 years. Global oil demand is growing by nearly 2% per year. Bearing these figures in mind, it is vital that we fully exploit the resources offered by the North Sea. This may mean over 400 production platforms in the North Sea, bringing a range of jobs to countries throughout Western Europe.

Representative from a major oil company

The EU operates the Common Fisheries Policy. This aims to manage resources to provide a balance between fish stocks and fishing activities. The Total Allowable Catch is set by the EU, but regulations must be maintained by the fishing industries and the member countries themselves. We are concerned about countries exceeding their quotas, and about the amount of fishing taking place by non-member countries.

Spokesperson for the European Union

Figure H   The viewpoints of some of those involved

▼ Questions

1 Why do you think that countries bordering the North Sea have used the sea to dump waste?
2 What are the main types of pollution which threaten the North Sea?
3 Why has over-fishing become such a problem?
4 A conference about the future of the North Sea is to be held in London. Imagine that you are present at the conference and have to report its main findings for a national newspaper. Before the conference, you are provided with the following information:

● An outline of items for discussion at the conference, with brief notes relating to each (see Figure G).
● A list of the countries taking part, and some of the organisations which will observe proceedings (see Figure F).
● The viewpoints of some of those involved (see Figure H).
● Background information (see pages 43–46).

Use all of the information given on these pages to produce your article, which should include:
a   a map or diagram showing countries bordering the North Sea;
b   a summary of the problems caused by pollution;
c   a summary of the problems caused by over-fishing;
d   some possible solutions;
e   an editorial comment, outlining your views on the future of the North Sea.
Your report could be word processed. ➡

Europe's changing economy

Key ideas & questions

- Economic conditions and levels of prosperity may change rapidly. How has the economy of Ireland changed in recent years?
- How have economic changes affected regional differences in Italy?
- What economic changes have taken place in eastern European countries, for example, Hungary and Poland, since the collapse of communism?
- **Transnational** companies like Fiat in Italy have a significant effect on economic development.
- Many countries of western Europe have a service dominated economy. In what ways is Belgium typical of this?

Main activity

Interpreting and designing advertisements. Researching into a transnational company, together with background questions on Hungary, Poland and Belgium.

CASE STUDY: Ireland – a changing economy

Figure A   Ireland

Figure B   Livestock farming dominates Irish agriculture

Do you know?

? Mild winds from the Atlantic mean that Ireland's winter temperatures are 14 °C higher than continental European locations on the same latitude.

? Since the election of a non-communist government in 1990, Hungary has attracted over $3.2 billion of foreign investment, more than the combined total for other eastern European countries.

? Poland's GNP dropped by nearly 20 % in the year following the collapse of the communist government.

? Fiat has 21 factories and research and development centres in South America.

Ireland is a country of mild temperatures and relatively high rainfall (see page 6). Situated on the western edge of Europe, its climate is greatly influenced by moist westerly winds and the warming effect of the North Atlantic Drift ocean current.

Farming has always been important in Ireland, accounting for 81 % of land use. Throughout the country, climatic conditions are suited to the rearing of livestock. The most fertile land, in the east and south, is where farms are largest and most productive. In 1995 there were over 7 million cattle in Ireland (compared with 3.5 million people!), contributing 90 % to the value of the country's agriculture. Meat and dairy products have long been important exports for Ireland.

Although physical conditions are suitable in many parts of Ireland, the production of crops is less important than livestock (see Figure C). In the European Union, for example, only Luxembourg and the Netherlands devote less land to cereal production than Ireland.

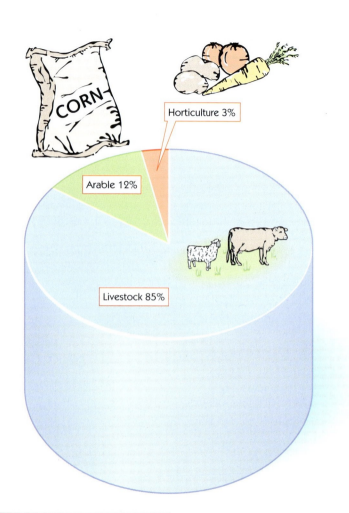

The Common Agricultural Policy (CAP) of the European Community encouraged farmers to increase production, giving guaranteed prices for unlimited quantities of farm products. As a result, by the late 1970s Irish and other European farmers were producing too much of some products, for example beef and milk. Changes to the CAP reduced surpluses, but also cut prices paid to farmers. The price of beef, for example, fell by 30 % between 1993 and 1996.

The decline in Irish agriculture has been matched by growth in other parts of the economy. Food and drink remain the major contributor, but hi-tech industries such as computer and software production, telecommunications and chemical manufacture are all areas of increasing importance (see Figure D). Ireland's second largest export, computer software, accounts for 60 % of all software imported by European countries. Ireland has been chosen as the centre for their European operations by computer transnationals such as Sun, Apple, Intel, and US Robotics.

Figure C   Agricultural land use in Ireland

Agriculture accounts for 8 % of Ireland's GNP, and employs nearly 14 % of the working population. This compares with an EU average of 2.8 % for GNP, employing 6 % of the workforce. Farming is clearly an important industry in Ireland, yet in recent years there has been a gradual decline in its importance to the country's economy.

This is a trend apparent throughout Europe; in 1980, 12 % of the working population of the European Community worked in agriculture. In Ireland, as elsewhere, there has been a decrease in agricultural employment as productivity has increased. Output has grown with the use of modern techniques and practices.

Figure D   The growth of hi-tech industries has transformed the Irish economy

Right now, two kinds of Java are hot in Cork. You could have found out whether anyone in Palo Alto has made it work yet without leaving your desk. But it was a nice evening. And downtown beckoned. ● So you followed the curving main street and let your nose lead you down a winding lane to where you're sitting now. Sipping the freshly roasted variety. Taking part in a lively argument distributed between Cambridge, Marin County and Patrick's Lane, Cork. ● Cork, you see, isn't just home to the Motorola European Software Development and Support Centre. It's a university town lining the banks of a river, with a healthy respect for its history as a merchant capital and its future as an interesting place to live and work in. ● Which brings us back to you. Motorola offers fresh challenges to people with good degrees in computer and electronic science. People willing to grow with us, as we expand. To travel. To take on responsibility for other people's performance, tackling one of the world's most advanced software engineering challenges in mobile communications, including GSM. ● We may have spoken before. Or we may have yet to meet. Either way, we'd like to hear from you. Send us an informative CV or e-mail the Human Resources Officer at TEI053@email.mot.com

Ⓜ **MOTOROLA**

Figure E Motorola, a transnational company expanding in Cork in Ireland

Growth in trade and prosperity

With a home market of only 3.5 million people, the Irish economy is heavily dependent upon trade. Industrialists are well aware of the importance of exploring new markets. Quick to adapt to market changes and new technology, the Irish economy has been transformed. Once a mainly agricultural society, in 1966 only 22 % of all exports were manufactured goods. This figure had risen to 71 % by 1996, with 80 % of manufacturing jobs involved with exports.

The United Kingdom is Ireland's main trading partner for both exports and imports. Although the value of exports to the UK has continued to increase in recent years, the proportion of total exports to that market has declined rapidly. This is due to a faster rate of increase in sales elsewhere, most notably to other countries in the EU. Expansion has also taken place in North

America and in newer markets such as Africa, Australia and the Far East.

In 1995 world trade grew by 8 %. In the same year, Irish trade growth was almost double this figure, making it one of the fastest growing economies in the world today. Government incentives have made Ireland an attractive location for overseas investment, increasing the pace of development and industrialisation.

Dublin – city and region

As a city and the centre of a region, Dublin is central to Ireland's growth and development (see Figure F). With a population of 1,025,000, Dublin has almost one-third of Ireland's total population. The city is the industrial and commercial centre of the country, and is the focal point for one of Ireland's growth industries, tourism.

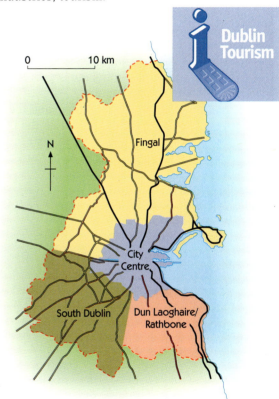

Figure F   Dublin county

Dublin has long been a famous centre for cultural or heritage holidays. The home of writers such as James Joyce and George Bernard Shaw, the city is one of the world's great literary centres. Dublin offers the tourist a wealth of attractions related to its cultural past and present (see Figure G). The city is used by tourists to visit other parts of Ireland. The Wicklow mountains, reaching over 920 metres in height, are to the south of the city. Galway, in the west of Ireland, is only 140 km from the capital.

The Georgian Trail
follows some of the most attractive Georgian Streets in the city south of the Liffey. It draws your attention principally to the features of that period but also to buildings and events of note from other times.

The Old City Trail
begins fittingly enough in College Green, where the Vikings built their Thing-mote and the 18th century parliament was located. All along the route are centres of power and influence that have shaped the history of Dublin.

The Cultural
The Four Courts, the and King's Inns - for described as "Gandon of the Liffey. This riety of culture a

Historical walking tours of Dublin

27 May - 29 September, 1996
Mon-Sat: 11am, 12 noon, and 3p
Sunday: 11am, 12 noon, 2pm an

Further info: 845 0241

October - May - winter schedule a
Booking necessary only for groups

DUBLIN BAY SEA THRILL

Dublin Bay Sea Thrill, East Pier, Dunlaoghaire, Co.
Tel/Fax: 2600949 Mobile: 087 5

For a Serious Adve
1 ¼ hour trip
7 days per week from Dunlaoghai

For lovers of exciting adventure and b
Dublin Bay Sea Thrill offers an experience b

Ride the waves and race the wind aboard 'The Th
wave hopping heart stopping ride around Dublin

It's a refreshing way to see the Dublin coastal area with
islands and marine life to bring you especially clo

• Optional Breakfast, Lunch and
Dinner in select venues including
18th Century Martello Tower
• Group rates / Credit cards
bookings available
• Ideal family activity

• The Thriller
licensed and
marine respe

• Tailor made cor
packages incl

TRINITY COLLEGE DUBLIN

The Dublin Experience
Your first stop when exploring Dublin, this audio-visual show tells the story of Dublin through the ages.
Daily, from 24th May to 30th September 10.00 to 17.00

The Book o
See the 9th C

Figure G   Dublin's numerous attractions include...

Monday - Saturday: 9.30 to 17.30 Sunday 12.00 to 17.00 Details of admission charges at entrance.

Although a growth industry, tourism still forms a minor part of the Irish economy, contributing below the EU average of 5 % of GNP. There are fewer than 1,000 hotels in Ireland, compared with 35,000 in Italy. Despite recent improvements, the quality of transport systems in Ireland is poorer than many other European countries. Parts of the country remain inaccessible, and the Irish government is trying, with help from the EU, to modernise the country's infrastructure. These improvements bring in more tourists, and benefit the economy as a whole.

Figure H   Grafton Street, Dublin city centre

Figure I   Taking traffic around the city centre, Dublin's streets are congested

Improved accessibility – Dublin's Northern Cross Motorway

Like any large city, the streets of Dublin's city centre are congested. The central shopping area of Grafton Street has been pedestrianised and is bordered by one-way streets (see Figure H). Journeys across the city are slow, with quick access to Dublin airport, 12 kilometres north of the city centre, being a major problem.

A new urban motorway, the M50, was proposed to solve some of Dublin's traffic problems. The scheme will eventually form a ring road around the outside of the city, and the latest section was opened in 1996 (see Figure J). This section, called the Northern Cross Motorway, links Dublin airport to most parts of the city via a fast road system. As well as benefiting industry and commuters, the new road system has improved access for visitors to the city.

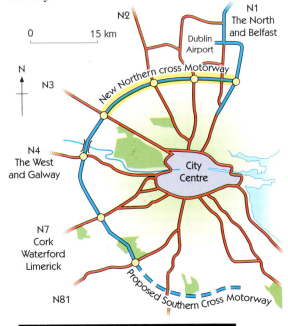

Figure J   The M50, Dublin's urban motorway

1 Why has farming always been important in Ireland? Refer to pages 6 and 7 in your answer.

▼ Questions

1 Why has farming always been important in Ireland? Refer to pages 6 and 7 in your answer.

2 What are the main reasons for the decline in farming in Ireland?

3 Look at Figure E taken from an Irish magazine.
   a   What type of people is the company trying to attract?
   b   Do you think it is aimed at local people? Give reasons for your answer.
   c   How does the advertisement try to encourage people to work in Cork?

4 Find an advertisement for a transnational company located in England, for example, in a national newspaper or magazine. What has the company done in order to attract potential workers?

5 Design an advert for a national newspaper in the United Kingdom to attract tourists to Ireland. You may choose a particular location, or type of holiday, or produce more general publicity. Your advert could be computer generated.

CASE STUDY: Change in eastern Europe

Do you know?

❓ At the fall of the communist government in Poland, the country owed $47 billion in foreign debt.

❓ Since the collapse of communism, foreign businesses have invested $5.5 billion in eastern Europe.

❓ Over $3.2 billion of this investment has been in Hungary alone.

Key ideas & questions

● After the Second World War the countries of eastern Europe were controlled by communist governments.
● These countries failed to match the economic progress of the west. This led to the collapse of communist governments at the end of the 1980s.
● The transition to a more western European style of economy has brought problems as well as benefits to east Europe.

The Second World War had a devastating effect upon eastern Europe. In Poland, for example, more than 6.5 million citizens had perished by the end of the war and much of the capital city of Warsaw was in ruins. Poland lost a total of 76,000 square kilometres to the Soviet Union, and much of the country's pre-war industry had been destroyed.

Figure A Unlike the First World War, where casualties and destruction were generally limited to battlefields, the Second World War saw devastation across the continent as a result of bombs, shelling and firestorms. Poland, and in particular Warsaw, were among the worst hit.

In the years following the war, communist governments controlled the countries of eastern Europe. As centrally planned economies, almost all important means of production, resources, transport and finance were run by the state. Private ownership was limited to agriculture and some service industries. Under communist rule, the development of heavy manufacturing industry became the priority (see Figure B). In Romania, for example, emphasis was placed on the development of machinery and chemical industries. A series of five year plans, based on the system used in the Soviet Union, neglected investment in agriculture and service industries. As a result, agricultural production suffered and there was a severe shortage of consumer goods.

By the 1970s, the communist economies of eastern Europe were in serious difficulty. In Poland, nearly three-quarters of farms remained in private ownership under communist rule. Inefficient agricultural production was unable to feed the Polish nation, leading to expensive imports. Crop yields in Poland were lower than anywhere else in eastern Europe. The problem was made worse by a series of bad harvests in the late 1970s, together with ageing technology and increasing price inflation.

In Hungary, the communist government attempted to transform the country's agriculture based economy. What little pre-war industry Hungary possessed was largely destroyed by 1945. The communist regime embarked on a programme of rapid industrialisation, again with the emphasis on heavy industries such as iron and steel. In common with other eastern European countries, this period of Hungary's industrial development paid little attention to the needs of the people. Environmental considerations were far less important then economic ones.

Figure B Industrial development in eastern Europe led to the development of heavy industry at the expense of the environment

By the 1980s the economic situation had grown worse throughout eastern Europe. Although countries such as Hungary had undergone some reforms, standards of living still lagged behind the levels of western Europe. In Romania, for example, the 1980s was a period of significant decline in all sectors of the economy. The country experienced a drop of approximately 5 % per year in its GNP.

By 1988, Poland had amassed foreign debts of more than $47 billion. It was largely as a result of such economic difficulties leading to public discontent that communist governments were overthrown at the end of the 1980s. Within a few years, former communist countries throughout eastern Europe had rejected the failure of the post-war years in favour of western style economies and democracy.

Instead of social and economic improvements, the former communist countries found the lack of state control caused immense difficulties. Government enterprises became private companies, many of the most profitable coming under foreign ownership. Without subsidies from the state, industries went bankrupt, or drastically reduced their workforces in order to remain competitive. As a result, unemployment levels soared, and industrial output declined. The GNP of Poland decreased by nearly 20 % during 1990–91, and price inflation rates in some parts of the former Soviet Union topped 1,000 % per year.

After the initial shock of change, the economies of eastern Europe have recovered (see Figure C) and moved towards further integration with western Europe. This is due in part to aid and development programmes drawn up by the European Union. The PHARE programme is one example, originally intended by the EU to provide aid for Hungary and Poland (see Figure D). By 1990, 12 countries were in receipt of aid through the PHARE programme, receiving a total of over 3 billion ECUs from the European Union.

Since the collapse of communism, most of the countries of eastern Europe have applied to join the EU (see pages 71–72). It is likely that, in the early years of the twenty-first century, the Union will spread eastwards across the continent. However, many problems remain on the road towards European integration. In particular, economic problems persist. Poland has received the largest contribution of aid from the EU, the greatest single contribution of 30 million ECUs being provided for agricultural development. Despite this, farming technology and productivity remains poor, and an obstacle to Poland joining the European Union. Most former communist countries are, as yet, nowhere near meeting the requirements for entry into the EU. With the growth in popularity in some countries of previous communist leaders, the stability of eastern Europe remains fragile.

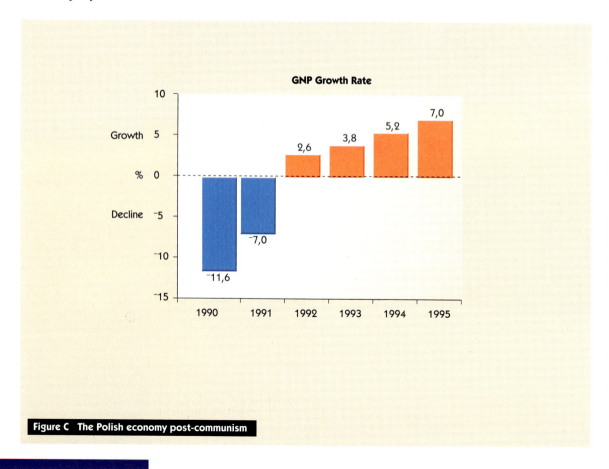

GNP Growth Rate

Figure C   The Polish economy post-communism

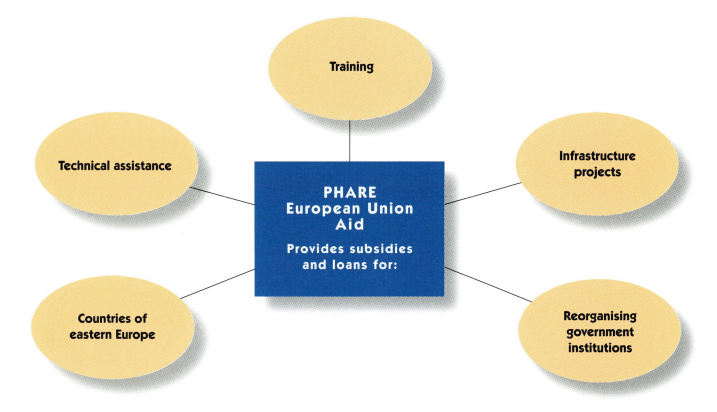

Figure D   PHARE is aid provided by the European Union to the countries of eastern Europe

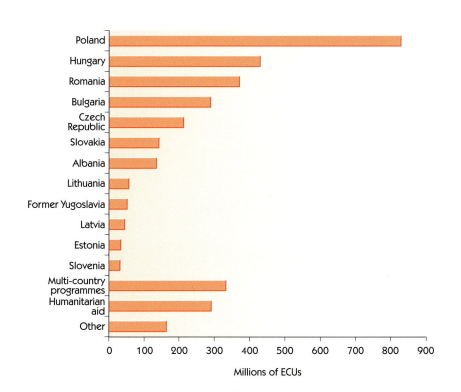

Millions of ECUs

Figure E   European Union aid to the former communist countries of eastern Europe

▼ Questions

1 What were the main features of communist rule in eastern Europe after the Second World War?

2 What problems did communist rule cause?

3 Why did the countries of eastern Europe experience problems after the collapse of communism?

4 What did the European Union do in order to solve these problems?

Review

Following the Second World War, the countries of eastern Europe were ruled by communist governments. These countries lagged behind the economic progress experienced in western Europe, leading to the collapse of communist rule. Economic reform has brought problems as well as benefits. Despite recent progress, most east European countries still fall short of the requirements for membership of the European Union.

FIAT

Fiat is the largest privately owned industry in Italy. The company directly employs nearly 237,000 people world-wide, operating in 60 countries. An estimated 450,000 people work in associated industries, such as dealers and suppliers. Fiat now challenges Volkswagen, the German car manufacturer, as Europe's leading car producer. Recent expansion has taken the Fiat group into China, the USA, Africa and Australia, making it a truly world-wide enterprise. In 1996, Fiat sold 2.3 million cars, as well as nearly 200,000 other vehicles. The importance of a transnational company like Fiat to the economy of Europe, and indeed the world, is shown in Figure A. The turnover generated by more than 200 factories exceeds the GNP of many nation states.

Fiat is an example of a transnational company which has expanded by diversifying into other types of manufacturing. Originally a manufacturer of cars, Fiat expanded rapidly after it was founded in 1899. By 1930, nearly two-thirds of the company's revenue came from foreign operations, a proportion which has remained steady until the present day. In addition to transport, the Fiat group is involved in areas as diverse as chemicals, bioengineering, and insurance services.

Economic activity is increasingly controlled by huge transnational corporations such as Fiat. Their products are made in many different countries, and sold throughout the world. This is known as **globalisation**. Transnationals locate throughout the world for three reasons:

1 To move their production nearer to large markets. In addition to meeting the needs of a local market, this will reduce the cost of transporting manufactured products.
2 To reduce the cost of importing raw materials and component parts.
3 To reduce the cost of labour. Wage rates are often significantly lower in the poorer countries favoured by transnationals.

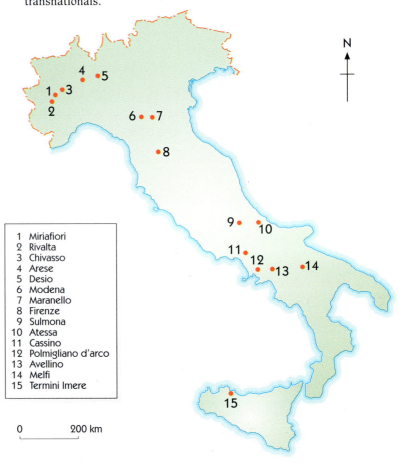

Country	Million US dollars per year
Sudan	11,000
Bangladesh	22,000
Bulgaria	22,000
Hungary	30,000
Ireland	33,000
Pakistan	42,000
Fiat	48,000
Poland	65,000
UK	930,000

1 Miriafiori
2 Rivalta
3 Chivasso
4 Arese
5 Desio
6 Modena
7 Maranello
8 Firenze
9 Sulmona
10 Atessa
11 Cassino
12 Polmigliano d'arco
13 Avellino
14 Melfi
15 Termini Imere

0   200 km

Figure A   Fiat's turnover is greater than the GNP of many countries

Figure B   Fiat production plants in Italy

Fiat in Italy

Fiat dominates the car industry in Italy. Other companies associated with the industry in Italy, such as Alfa Romeo, Ferrari, Masarati and Lancia, work with or are owned by Fiat, which produces nearly three-quarters of the cars made in Italy. Unlike many other European car manufacturers, Fiat is not controlled by foreign companies. From its original base in Turin, Fiat has spread throughout Italy (see Figure B). Many of the company's factories are specialised, producing components which are then transported to other factories for assembly. In addition to the industrialised north of the country, Fiat has built factories in the poorer south, or Mezzogiorno. With good access to the Italian motorway network, government help has made such a location attractive to many industries.

Fiat's most recently constructed factory at Melfi (see Figure C) shows the increasing importance of environmental considerations in manufacturing industries. The factory, near Naples, produces about 400,000 vehicles per year. It has been designed to fit in with the environment as far as possible, and to minimise pollution. Most of the 25,000 tonnes of waste produced each year is processed within the factory. Where possible materials are recycled, for example, 80 % of the water is reused. Waste which cannot be used again is burnt, the heat produced being used to generate electricity. Melfi incinerates waste from other Fiat factories, and from other industries in the local area.

Fiat in Europe

Fiat is one of Europe's leading motor manufacturers, accounting for 11 % of the cars sold in western Europe in 1995. In addition to Italy, it has plants in eight other European countries (see Figure D). Well established in EU countries, Fiat has moved into eastern Europe, with 10 factories situated in Poland. The growth of Fiat's range of products is evident in its European operations. The Polish plants are the only ones outside Italy that produce cars. Elsewhere, products as various as tractors, heart-lung machines and artificial fibres are produced.

Figure C The environmental challenge

In the United Kingdom, Fiat controls 25 companies, employing over 7,000 people. The £2 billion generated by Fiat UK makes a significant contribution to the group's annual turnover. During the 1980s and early 1990s, Britain emerged as a leading destination for foreign investment, and Fiat proved to be a major player in this field. By 1991, mergers and takeovers had seen the group's UK enterprise grow to include 10 locations in England, including the world headquarters in London of New Holland, tractor makers bought by Fiat from Ford.

The five research and development centres in the UK form part of a world-wide network which employs 14,000 people. Fiat spends over £2 billion annually in order to remain competitive. Research into alternative fuel systems, for example, has led to the development of vehicles powered by electricity or compressed natural gas. Robots, supercomputers and new factories account for a further £3 billion. In total, approximately 10 % of the group's income is spent on development for the future. Today automobiles account for 49 % of total Fiat group turnover.

Switzerland	United Kingdom	France	Germany
1 Neuhausen	1 Manchester	1 Arras	1 Nemünster
2 Bedano	2 Cannock	2 Amiens	2 Cottbus
	3 Birmingham	3 Caen	3 Heilbronn
	4 Langley	4 Chalon	4 Freiburg
	5 Basildon	5 Argentan	5 Weisweil
	6 Coventry	6 Chatellerault	6 Ulm
		7 Dieuze	7 Ludwigstadt
Portugal		8 Strasbourg	8 Munich
1 Arganil		9 Coex	
		10 Bourbon Lancy	
Spain		11 Lyon	Poland
1 Bilbao		12 Valence	1 Twadogora
2 Logroño		13 St Aubin	2 Dabrowa Gornicza
3 Valladolid			3 Sosnowiec
4 Gaudalajara			4 Tychy
5 Madrid			5 Skoczow
6 Blanes	Belgium		6 Czechowice
7 Barcelona	1 Antwerp		7 Bielsko Biala
8 Mataró	2 Zedelgem		

Figure D   Fiat in Europe

▼ Questions

1 a What is a transnational company?
   b Why do transnationals locate in countries throughout the world?

2 Why is Fiat such an important industry to Italy?

3 Write a report on Fiat as an example of a transnational company. Your report should include the following sections:
   a a map to show the location of headquarters and factories in Italy;
   b detail on the location of overseas branches;
   c a written account of the growth and development of the company;
   d the main products sold, with reference to diversification;
   e sales and profit figures.

4 Make a list of other transnational companies, to cover a range of manufacturing industries (for example food production, chemical industries etc.)
   In a small group, research one of these companies. Use your school library and other resources (for example the school's Business department) to find out information about your chosen company.
   Contact the company and ask for general information. Companies like Fiat may be contacted at their UK headquarters by post, phone/fax, or by e-mail (Fiat's home page, for example, is www.fiat.com).
   When you have collected your information, write a report with a similar structure to that for Fiat. Include a section outlining similarities and differences between the two companies. ➡

5 Give a presentation of the results of your research to the rest of the class.

Europe's economy – the growth in services

The economic structure of the European Union has changed fundamentally in the last 30 years. In 1970, secondary industries contributed 42 % to the Gross National Product of the Community. Although this figure hides differences both between and within member states, manufacturing industries dominated employment as a whole.

By 1996, there had been a decline in employment in both primary and secondary industries. Even in the peripheral areas of the EU, agriculture employed fewer and fewer people. Ireland and Portugal, examples used elsewhere, illustrate this trend. Population movement away from rural areas in search of improved employment and living conditions left fewer people to work on farms. In the United Kingdom, 5 % of the working population were employed in primary industries in 1970. This figure had declined to 3 % by 1996 (with 1.2 % in agriculture), a result of continued improvements in the productivity and efficiency of farming.

This decline has been matched by the fall in employment in manufacturing industries. Throughout Europe, traditional manufacturing regions have struggled in the face of competition from overseas, and industries have cut their labour force to remain in business. The United Kingdom has seen employment in secondary industries fall from 46 % to 25 % in 30 years.

Throughout the European Union, as with other industrialised nations, the growth area has been in service industries (see Figure A), both in terms of employment and GNP. Nearly two-thirds of the EU's wealth is generated by service industries, and the figure is continuing to rise. The biggest growth has been in market or business services, providing support for other economic activities (see Figure B).

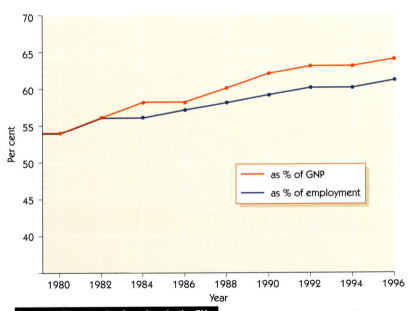

Figure A The growth of services in the EU

as % of GNP
as % of employment

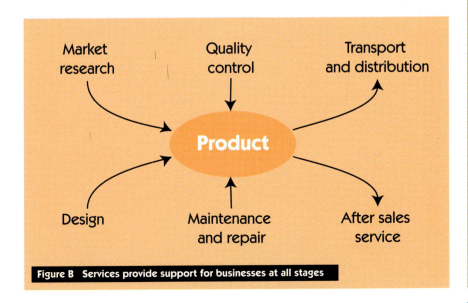

Figure B Services provide support for businesses at all stages

Market research

Quality control

Transport and distribution

Product

Design

Maintenance and repair

After sales service

The pattern of employment in service industries in the EU is complex, showing marked variations within individual countries (see Figure C). Overall, the growth of services in the EU is due to the following:

1. The increasing efficiency of manufacturing industry. This means that industries create more wealth, giving people more money to spend. With the working week becoming shorter, more of this money is spent on leisure, entertainment, and other services.
2. As manufacturing industries become more efficient, they require fewer workers to produce their goods. Many people have found alternative employment in service industries.
3. The population of Europe, particularly countries in the west, is ageing. An increasing proportion of the population is of retirement age, requiring the provision of services such as long-term medical care and leisure services.

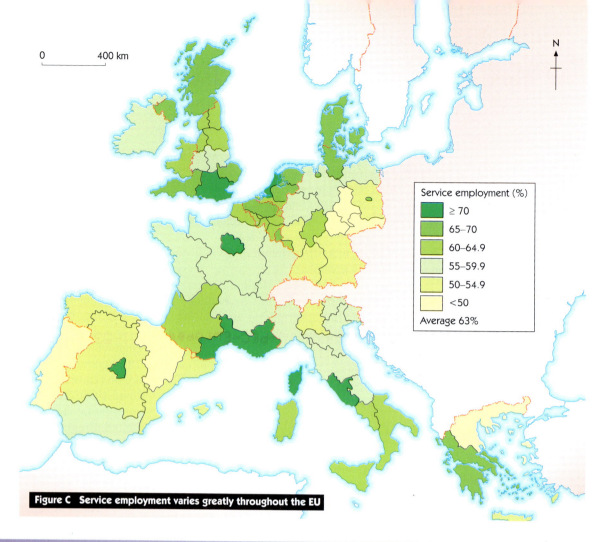

Service employment (%)

- ≥ 70
- 65–70
- 60–64.9
- 55–59.9
- 50–54.9
- <50

Average 63%

Figure C   Service employment varies greatly throughout the EU

CASE STUDY: Belgium – a service dominated economy

Figure D   The location of Belgium

This case study illustrates the decline in manufacturing and growth in service industries which is typical of Western European countries.

Belgium is one of the smallest countries in Europe, with one of the highest population densities. The country's 10 million people occupy a land area of 35,000 square kilometres, at an average density of 323 people per square kilometre. The capital city of Brussels has a population of just under one million. It is the base for a large number of international organisations including the European Commission and NATO, and over 1,500 transnational companies. One-third of Belgium's population lives in the country's industrial towns and cities, of which Antwerp and Ghent are the largest. The narrow industrial corridor between Mons and Charleroi is also densely populated. Belgium is one of the most urbanised countries in the world, with 97 % of its population living in towns and cities.

Despite its small population, Belgium has one of the highest GNP levels in Europe. Until recently, much of the country's wealth was derived from its industrial products (see Figure E). A decline in manufacturing output has been matched by a steady growth in service industries. Over two-thirds of the working population is employed in service industries, one of the highest in Europe (see Figure F).

Figure E Employment in manufacturing industries has declined, although Belgium still profits from the processing of imported raw materials. Service industries dominate Brussels, an international administrative centre.

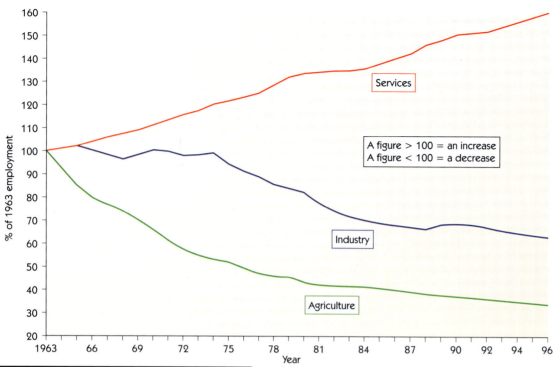

Figure F   Belgium's changing employment structure

A figure > 100 = an increase
A figure < 100 = a decrease

The Belgium–Luxembourg Economic Union (BLEU)

In 1992 Belgium and Luxembourg renewed the agreement to join their economies, first made in 1921, for a further 10 years. The two countries form a single area for most purposes. They combine their wealth, and share a single customs area. Although each country issues its own currency, the Belgian and Luxembourg Francs are worth exactly the same as each other. The two countries are heavily dependent upon international trade, exporting more per person than any other country in western Europe.

	% Primary	% Secondary	% Tertiary
Albania	55	20	25
Poland	28	35	37
Hungary	25	22	53
Ireland	13	57	30
Spain	11	34	55
Italy	8	33	59
France	7	29	64
Germany	3	40	57
Belgium	3	30	67
United Kingdom	3	25	72

Figure G   The employment structure of various European countries

▼ Questions

1 Describe the ways in which economic structures have changed in Europe in the last 30 years.

2 Give reasons for these differences.

3 Write a Fact File on Belgium. Include the main features of the country and its economy. (You could include detail from reference books, CD Roms, and the Internet.)

4 Figure G shows the employment structure for various European countries. Draw a triangular graph to show these figures. Describe and explain the pattern shown on your completed graph.

Shrinking Europe

Main activity

Questions relating to the effects of the Channel Tunnel

Key ideas & questions

● Improved transport networks have increased accessibility in some parts of the European Union.
● The European Union is planning trans-European transport systems to be in place early in the twenty-first century.
● The Channel Tunnel is an important part of Europe's transport network. It has cut journey times between the United Kingdom and the rest of Europe.

The development of high speed rail networks and a trans-European road network is planned for the following reasons:

● To create quick access from one country to another, particularly since the creation of the single market for trading in the EU. In particular, this involves the building of cross-border roads or motorways.
● To fill in gaps in the network, and to unblock bottlenecks in the present system.
● The need to make the peripheral regions of Europe more accessible to the main roads that carry 75 % of Europe's total freight traffic. To this end, trans-European road links are planned to extend towards Mediterranean Europe and to the former communist countries of the east (see Figure A).
● Efficient transport creates wealth. Commercial transport contributes 5 % of the European Union's GNP, and the rapid transfer of goods and services will increase trade within and beyond the EU.

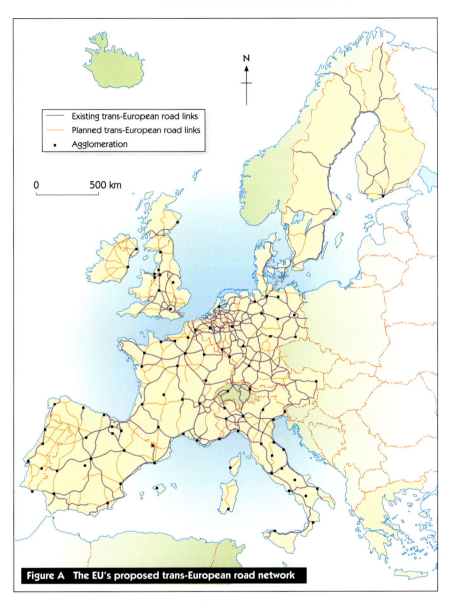

Existing trans-European road links
Planned trans-European road links
■ Agglomeration

0   500 km

Figure A   The EU's proposed trans-European road network

Figure B   A fast and frequent service enables vehicles to cross the English channel in 35 minutes

Do you know?

? Commercial transport employs approximately 5 % of the EU's working population.
? Transport as a whole accounts for over 30 % of energy used in Europe.
? The European Union has one of the most advanced, complex and dense transport networks in the world. The standard and efficiency of transport systems varies greatly throughout the continent. The completion of Europe-wide transport networks is one of the EU's top priorities, for which a budget of 20 billion ECUs per year is allocated.

Figure C The terminal at Cheriton, near Folkestone. The shuttle track is built in a loop to enable trains to provide a continuous service. Unlike the Calais terminal which was virtually a greenfield site, the English terminal has had to be screened from local housing. Earth embankments and 500,000 trees and shrubs have been used for this purpose.

The Channel Tunnel was officially opened in May 1994. The Tunnel operates a cross-channel rail service for private and goods vehicles called 'Le Shuttle' (see Figure B). Journey times across the English Channel are only 35 minutes, with quick entry into and departure from the terminals. The speed of access and short journey time are competition for other carriers, particularly the cross-channel ferries.

The Tunnel also carries trains on route to other destinations, with its 'Eurostar' service. The rail tracks that run through the Tunnel are linked to the main British and French rail networks. This means that trains are able to pass straight through without stopping at the terminals. Eurostar takes just over three hours to complete the journey from London to Brussels.

The Channel Tunnel is an important part of Europe's transport network, linking the United Kingdom to the rest of the continent. The Tunnel forms part of a network of high speed rail links due to be completed by 2010 (see Figure D). Some links, for example from the Channel Tunnel to Paris, are already in operation. Travelling at speeds of up to 295 km/h, the rail network will dramatically reduce journey times throughout Europe. Only eight hours after emerging from the Tunnel on French territory, a traveller could be in Berlin, Milan or Barcelona.

▼ Questions

1 Look at Figure D. Using the high-speed rail network, how long would it take to travel from London to:
   a Paris?
   b Berlin?
   c Rome?

2 What effect do you think the Channel Tunnel will have upon the European economic 'core'? (See pages 61–62). Give reasons for your answer.

3 Figure C shows the Channel Tunnel terminal near Folkestone. What environmental problems do you think a development of this scale could cause?

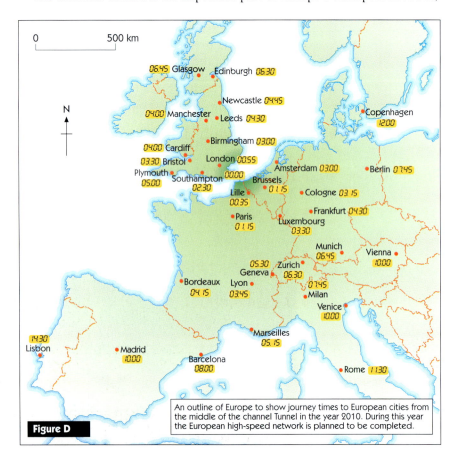

An outline of Europe to show journey times to European cities from the middle of the channel Tunnel in the year 2010. During this year the European high-speed network is planned to be completed.

Figure D

Review

Transport is an important industry in the European Union. The standard of transport systems varies across the continent, and the EU is planning the development of trans-European road and rail links to promote economic development. The Channel Tunnel is an important element in the proposed high speed European rail network. The Tunnel has cut journey times between the United Kingdom and the rest of Europe.

Core and periphery in Europe

Main activity

An analysis of different levels of development within Europe.

Key ideas & questions

● Standards of living and quality of life vary both between and within countries.

● It is possible to identify core and peripheral regions in Europe.

● Are Italy and Germany at the core of Europe? Is Portugal a typical country on the periphery of Europe?

CASE STUDY: The European core – Italy and Germany

Levels of economic development vary from one country to another. There may also be differing levels of prosperity between regions within a country. Is it possible to identify a European 'core' area, and countries which occupy the 'periphery'?

Germany and Italy – European core region?

Germany, bordered by nine countries, is situated at the heart of Europe. The country not only links east and west Europe, but also links Scandinavia with the Mediterranean. In such a central location, and with a population second only in Europe to Russia, it is not surprising that Germany has become the economic core of Europe.

Since the end of the Second World War Germany has grown to its current position as one of the world's leading industrial nations. In terms of Gross National Product, the indicator most frequently used to measure a nation's wealth, Germany currently ranks third in the world (see Figure B).

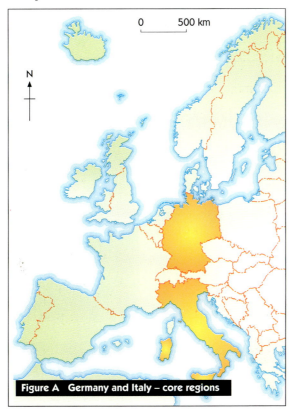

Figure A Germany and Italy – core regions

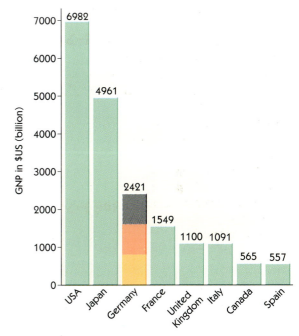

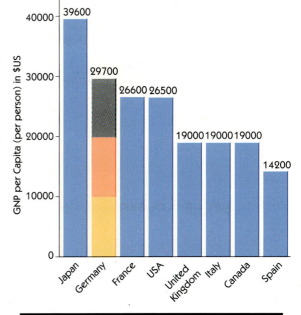

Figure B Germany ranks among the world's wealthiest nations

Do you know?

? Funds provided for regional development by the EU come from money provided by all member states. This money is called the European Union's budget.

? In 1995 the EU budget came to 76 billion ECUs. This is equivalent to 1.2 % of the total GNP of member countries, or 205 ECUs per person.

The basis of the country's wealth is its manufacturing industries, which employ over one-third of the working population. The most important industrial region is in North Rhine-Westphalia, which includes the steel producing Ruhr area (see Figure C). Germany's leading industrial products are chemicals, transport equipment (the country is the world's third largest car producer) and machinery.

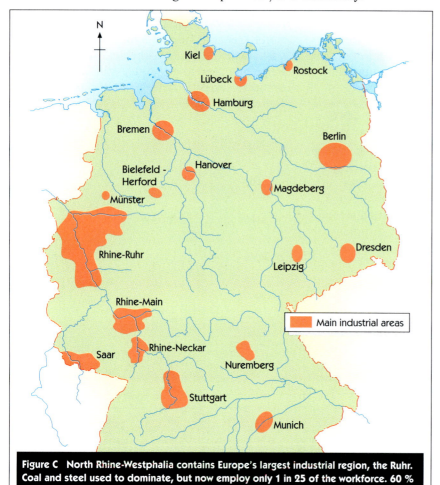

Figure C North Rhine-Westphalia contains Europe's largest industrial region, the Ruhr. Coal and steel used to dominate, but now employ only 1 in 25 of the workforce. 60 % work in services.

Social and economic indicators:	Germany	Italy	Portugal
Population density (per sq km)	228	190	110
Birth rate (per 000)	10	10	12
Death rate (per 000)	12	10	11
Urban population (%)	86	67	30
Adult literacy (%)	99	98	86
Energy consumption (kg oil equivalent per person)	4,054	2,820	1,463
GNP ($US per person)	29,700	19,000	7,890
Working population employed in agriculture (%)	5	7	12

Figure D Indicators of wealth

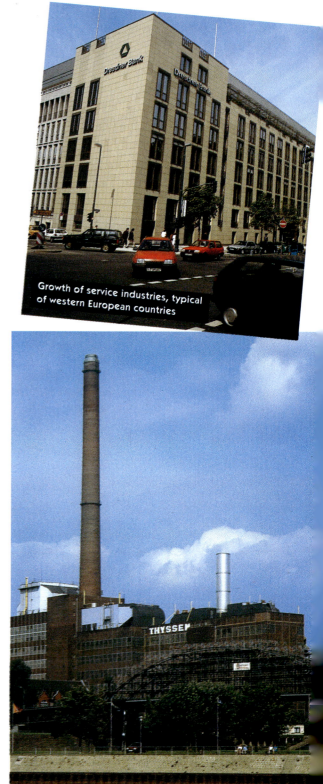

Growth of service industries, typical of western European countries

Figure E Germany's wealth is based on manufacturing

Figure D shows some commonly used indicators of social and economic development. Compare the figures for Germany and Italy. Although Italy has a high GNP figure per capita (per person), there are still enormous differences in wealth between the north and south of the country.

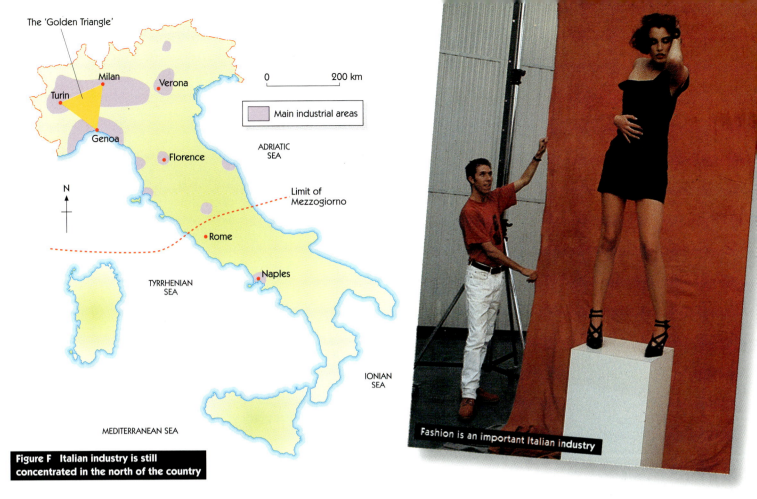

Figure F Italian industry is still concentrated in the north of the country

Fashion is an important Italian industry

The north of Italy remains the richest, containing most of the industry that generates over half of the country's wealth (see Figure F). The south of Italy, the *Mezzogiorno*, still has the lowest GNP figures and the highest agricultural employment in Italy. Unemployment figures are higher than the national average, and the area still suffers from migration to the north of the country. Government investment in the south in the 1950s and 60s provided better transport and communication, but industrial investment remained limited.

More recently, Italy has received money from the European Union. The regions of the south have received grants to help with road and rail projects, public services, and to encourage industries to locate in the south. Italy has received more regional aid from the European Union than any other country. Despite the decision of companies such as Fiat to locate in the south (see pages 54–56), the gap between the two halves of Italy remains great (see Figure G). To what extent is Italy a part of the European economic core, or should only northern Italy be considered the core?

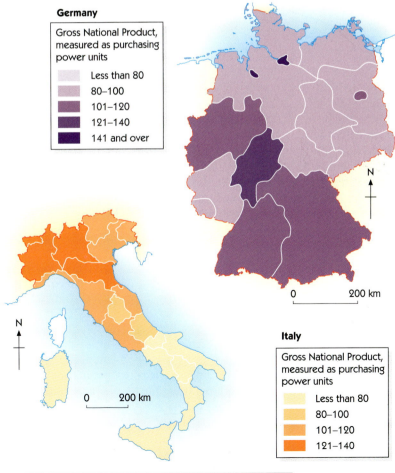

Figure G The regional distribution of GNP in Germany and Italy

Legend:
- Regions of lagging development
- Industrial areas in decline
- Rural areas under development

0   500 km

N

Glasgow
Tyneside
Dublin
Leeds
Manchester
Birmingham
London
Copenhagen
Hamburg
Amsterdam
Berlin
Brussels
Lille
Cologne
Paris
Luxembourg
Munich
Bordeaux
Lyons
Turin
Milan
Bilbao
Toulouse
Geneva
Zaragoza
Marseilles
Madrid
Barcelona
Lisbon
Valencia
Rome
Seville
Naples
Thessaloniki
Málaga
Palmero
Athens

Figure H   The distribution of EU regional aid

EU Regional Policies

The European Union has a range of measures which are designed to help poorer member states. Together with money from national governments, the EU provides assistance for areas with particular problems. Financial help is given to any region meeting one or more of six community Objectives, with 1, 2, and 5 being of a specifically regional nature. A map of regions qualifying for EU assistance under these Objectives (Figure H) shows the nature of the European core and periphery, and how the Structural Funds aim to ensure balanced economic and social development. Developments are seen as a partnership between the EU and national governments, with the money provided by the Structural Funds being matched by the member state (see Figure I).

Objective 1 regions, areas of lagging development, have a GNP per capita less than 75 % of the EU average. These are the peripheral regions of the community where there is little industry, or where industry is threatened. As well as the whole of Ireland,

Greece and Portugal, the former East Germany and most of Spain fall into this category. Priorities for development in these regions include manufacturing, communications, energy and water supply, and research and development. More than one quarter of the population of the EU live in these regions.

The areas targeted by **Objective 2** rely heavily upon manufacturing, but are experiencing industrial decline leading to high levels of unemployment. Often with a smaller scale focus, the list of regions is revised every three years. The priority in these areas is the creation of employment, and the quality of the industrial environment.

Objective 5 is concerned with the development of rural areas. These areas have a large proportion of jobs in agriculture, low population density, and often experience loss of population. The focus here is on creating a range of employment outside agriculture, particularly in small and medium-sized businesses.

Allocation of EU structure funds, 1994–1999

Country	Objective 1 (lagging development)	Objective 2 (declining industry)	Objective 5 (rural areas)
Belgium	730	160	77
Denmark	–	56	54
Germany	13,640	733	1,227
Greece	13,980	–	–
Spain	26,300	1,130	664
France	2,190	1,765	2,238
Ireland	5,620	–	–
Italy	14,860	684	901
Luxembourg	–	7	6
The Netherlands	150	300	150
Austria	184	n/a	n/a
Portugal	13,980	–	–
Finland	–	n/a	n/a
Sweden	–	n/a	n/a
United Kingdom	2,360	2,142	817

Figure I Funds allocated by the European Union (million ECUs)

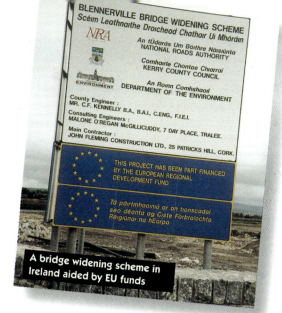

A bridge widening scheme in Ireland aided by EU funds

Core and periphery – Europe's 'hot banana'

European Union planners have mapped the area they consider to be the European economic core. The result is a banana shaped area which stretches from south-east England through western Germany to northern Italy (see Figure I). Planners predict that the so-called 'hot banana' will attract more investment and wealth in the early years of the twenty-first century. This is likely to increase problems in peripheral areas such as Portugal, southern Italy and Greece.

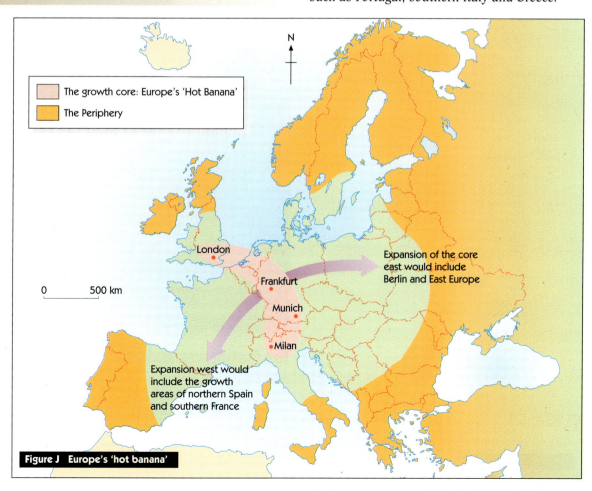

The growth core: Europe's 'Hot Banana'

The Periphery

London

Frankfurt

Munich

Milan

Expansion of the core east would include Berlin and East Eorpe

Expansion west would include the growth areas of northern Spain and southern France

0 500 km

Figure J Europe's 'hot banana'

Portugal is a country on the edge of Europe, together with Spain forming the Iberian peninsula in the extreme south-west of the continent (see Figure K). Population density is highest in the coastal strip between Lisbon and Oporto, where the country's economic activity is concentrated. Out of the total population of 10 million people, 40 % live in this region, with two million in the greater Lisbon area and 1,630,000 in the Oporto conurbation. Much of the rest of Portugal is sparsely populated, with only 30 % of the population living in urban areas.

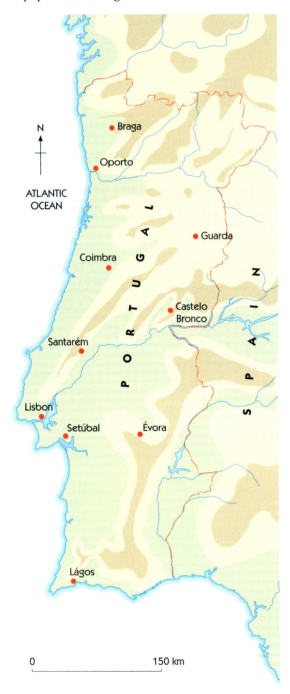

Figure L   Portugal, like Germany and Italy, has regional differences in income. One disadvantage of EU aid is that it has tended to benefit urban and wealthy areas at the expense of the poor.

Figure K   The location of Portugal

The Portuguese economy

Agriculture has always been important to the economy of Portugal. In 1985 26 % of the country's workforce were employed in primary industries. In addition to wine, olive oil and potatoes, Portugal is one of the world's leading producers of cork (40 % of Portugal is forested). Manufactured goods include processed food, textiles and machinery, although Portugal still relies heavily upon imports.

In 1975 the Portuguese government took control of many of the country's major industries, including financial institutions, transport, and telecommunications. Many of these enterprises became inefficient, and performed poorly in comparison with other European countries. The Portuguese economy remained dominated by agriculture, which employed nearly one-third of the total workforce.

Portugal and the European Union

Portugal became a member of the European Community (now the European Union) in 1986. Membership of the Community had a major impact on the Portuguese economy. This arose from:

1 Easier access to European markets, with a total population of over 370 million. In 1989, the value of Portuguese exports grew by 25 %, compared with a 2 % decline in 1981.
2 Many state owned enterprises were privatised after 1986, in an attempt to introduce more competition into Portuguese industry. In 1987 publicly owned businesses contributed 20 % to Portugal's GNP. This had decreased to 10 % by 1995, with further decreases planned by 2000.
3 Increased investment from abroad. Before joining the European Community, Portugal was seen as a country which offered few incentives and many barriers to foreign industries. The privatisations of the late 1980s greatly increased competition and efficiency, making Portugal more attractive for foreign businesses. Between 1980 and 1991, investment from abroad rose from £53 million to a peak of £1,337 million.
4 The availability of assistance through the EU Structure funds. The whole of Portugal qualifies for funding from the European Union as an underdeveloped region. The country has been allocated 14 billion ECUs to spend by the end of the century.

In many ways, the Portuguese economy has been transformed since the country joined the European Union. Agricultural employment has declined, and is now more in line with other western European countries (see Figure M). Foreign investment in the country has increased, taking advantage of low wage rates and EU incentives. As a result, Portugal has become the base for many transnational companies to manufacture and export goods. Service industries have grown in importance, and tourism now makes a substantial contribution to Portugal's national wealth (see Figure N).

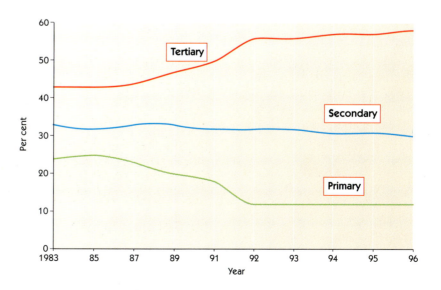

Figure M Portugal's changing employment structure

Figure N   Tourism contributes over $2 billion to the Portuguese economy each year

GNP has risen substantially since 1986, but remains only 64 % of the EU average. By many social and economic indicators, Portugal lags behind other western European nations. For example, at 86 % adult literacy rates are among the lowest in the continent, and Portugal remains one of the economically least developed countries of the European Union.

▼ Questions

1 Look at Figure D which gives indicators about Germany, Italy and Portugal. Find out the same information for the other member states of the EU.

2 Using Figure D complete two choropleth (density shading) maps of the European Union. Draw one to show the percentage figures for urban population and another to show the percentage of population working in agriculture. Remember to choose the categories for each map carefully, which should be drawn using different shades of one colour.

3 Draw a scattergraph to show the relationship between GNP and any one other indicator. Remember to draw a line of best fit, and that the GNP figures should be drawn using the horizontal or 'x' axis.

4 Using your maps and graph, together with information from the text, answer the following questions:

a   Which countries in the European Union appear to be the most developed?

b   Which countries appear to be the least developed?

c   Is it true to say that there is a big difference in wealth between the richest and poorest countries in the EU?

5 Find out similar information about countries in eastern Europe. How do the poorest members of the European Union compare with these? ➡

Review

Levels of economic development vary both between and within countries. It has been suggested that the core of Europe is a zone stretching from south-east England to north Italy. Germany and Italy show many features typical of an economic core, yet both countries have significant regional differences in wealth.

The European Union provides assistance for poorer regions of the community. Italy has received the greatest share of funds, mostly to aid development in the south of the country. Portugal is, in many ways, typical of a peripheral region. Despite much economic progress since joining the EU in 1986, Portugal remains among the poorest countries in Europe.

Europe in change

Key ideas & questions

- Economic development is linked to decisions taken by international unions and agreements, such as the European Union.
- How have political changes in eastern Europe affected economic development in the Baltic States of Lithuania, Estonia and Latvia?

Main activity

Analysing change in the Baltic region and comparing the problems of the Baltic with the North Sea.

Europe, a continent of great contrasts and over 30 countries, has never been politically united. Since the end of the Second World War, much of the continent has experienced peace, prosperity, and a high quality of life. The aftermath of the war led to the formation of the European Community in 1957, in an attempt to ensure economic co-operation in Europe. The United Kingdom joined the six original member states in 1973, since when the Community has continued to expand across Europe.

The economic success of the Community, now called the European Union, has seen the size of the organisation treble in the past 40 years (see Figure A). Having grown from 6 to 15 members

by 1995, the Union faces the challenge of enlargement to 20 or even 30 countries in the near future.

This economic growth and prosperity enjoyed by some countries has not been apparent throughout the continent. The 'Iron Curtain' of the post-war years separated nearly 300 million people from the economic successes of western

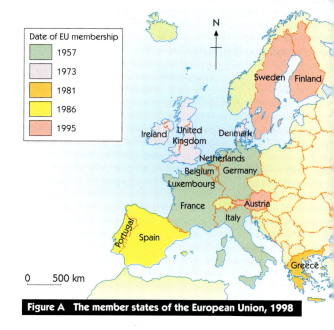

Date of EU membership	
	1957
	1973
	1981
	1986
	1995

0   500 km

Figure A   The member states of the European Union, 1998

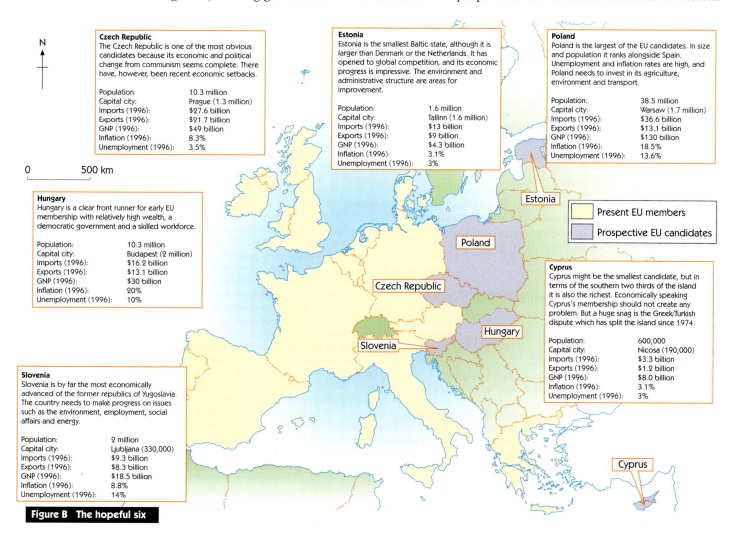

Czech Republic
The Czech Republic is one of the most obvious candidates because its economic and political change from communism seems complete. There have, however, been recent economic setbacks.

Population:	10.3 million
Capital city:	Prague (1.3 million)
Imports (1996):	$27.6 billion
Exports (1996):	$21.7 billion
GNP (1996):	$49 billion
Inflation (1996):	8.3%
Unemployment (1996):	3.5%

Estonia
Estonia is the smallest Baltic state, although it is larger than Denmark or the Netherlands. It has opened to global competition, and its economic progress is impressive. The environment and administrative structure are areas for improvement.

Population:	1.6 million
Capital city:	Tallinn (1.6 million)
Imports (1996):	$13 billion
Exports (1996):	$9 billion
GNP (1996):	$4.3 billion
Inflation (1996):	3.1%
Unemployment (1996):	3%

Poland
Poland is the largest of the EU candidates. In size and population it ranks alongside Spain. Unemployment and inflation rates are high, and Poland needs to invest in its agriculture, environment and transport.

Population:	38.5 million
Capital city:	Warsaw (1.7 million)
Imports (1996):	$36.6 billion
Exports (1996):	$13.1 billion
GNP (1996):	$130 billion
Inflation (1996):	18.5%
Unemployment (1996):	13.6%

Hungary
Hungary is a clear front runner for early EU membership with relatively high wealth, a democratic government and a skilled workforce.

Population:	10.3 million
Capital city:	Budapest (2 million)
Imports (1996):	$16.2 billion
Exports (1996):	$13.1 billion
GNP (1996):	$30 billion
Inflation (1996):	20%
Unemployment (1996):	10%

Cyprus
Cyprus might be the smallest candidate, but in terms of the southern two thirds of the island it is also the richest. Economically speaking Cyprus's membership should not create any problem. But a huge snag is the Greek/Turkish dispute which has split the island since 1974.

Population:	600,000
Capital city:	Nicosa (190,000)
Imports (1996):	$3.3 billion
Exports (1996):	$1.2 billion
GNP (1996):	$8.0 billion
Inflation (1996):	3.1%
Unemployment (1996):	3%

Slovenia
Slovenia is by far the most economically advanced of the former republics of Yugoslavia. The country needs to make progress on issues such as the environment, employment, social affairs and energy.

Population:	2 million
Capital city:	Ljubljana (330,000)
Imports (1996):	$9.3 billion
Exports (1996):	$8.3 billion
GNP (1996):	$18.5 billion
Inflation (1996):	8.8%
Unemployment (1996):	14%

	Present EU members
	Prospective EU candidates

0   500 km

Figure B   The hopeful six

Short-listing of Cyprus angers spurned Turkey

Five former communist countries from central and eastern Europe yesterday celebrated having passed the first hurdle on the road towards becoming full members of the European Union next century.

In an historic announcement to the European Parliament in Strasbourg, Jacques Santer declared that Poland, Hungary, the Czech Republic, Slovenia and Estonia had, along with Cyprus, all achieved the necessary economic and political reforms to allow negotiations to open in January.

Although heads of EU governments will have to approve the plan at a summit in December, the commission announcement raises the prospect of EU membership growing from 15 to at least 21 by 2004.

But the delight of successful applicants was in contrast to other countries left disappointed. Lithuania, Latvia, Romania, Bulgaria and Slovakia all had their applicants rejected. In a foretaste of the diplomatic battles that will accompany the enlargement process, the Commission immediately faced the wrath of excluded Turkey, claiming that Cyprus should not be allowed to join the EU until a solution was reached in the conflict over its divided status.

Figure C   From the Daily Telegraph 17 July 1997, EU expansion

Europe. It is the collapse of communism in eastern Europe which has quickened the pace of change in recent years. How will these countries of eastern Europe cope with new ways of economic and political management? How will border disputes be solved? How will ethnic tensions be dealt with? Will the newly formed democracies survive?

The EU is likely to become a stabilising factor in such a rapidly changing situation. European unity and co-operation will depend to a large extent upon how successfully eastern European states are included in organisations established by the European Union. Recent negotiations will probably see the eastward expansion of the EU in the early years of next century (see Figures B and C).

In addition to full membership, a number of agreements have been put into place to strengthen links between the EU and eastern European countries. Yet, extending the EU brings problems as well as benefits. New member states would require massive support for agriculture and regional development, more than could be afforded by the present budget. The administration of the Union is difficult enough without extra countries placing further strain upon the system.

The break-up of the Soviet Union has caused rapid change along Europe's eastern border. The effects of the past, and the uncertain future facing Europe's changing states is illustrated by the Baltic States of Lithuania, Estonia and Latvia.

CASE STUDY: The Baltic

Europe's North-east frontier

The Baltic states

The Baltic region contains 50 million people and some of Europe's larger cities (see Figure D). Dominated until recently by the powers of Germany and the Soviet Union, the Baltic became an economic and political divide between east and west. The rapid political changes which have reshaped the countries of central and eastern Europe have had a dramatic effect upon the Baltic area.

Figure D   The Baltic region contains some of Europe's larger cities, for example Stockholm

Under Soviet rule, the Baltic states were given specific economic roles. Lithuania, for example, manufactured televisions for the whole of the USSR. Though poor by western European standards, the states achieved three of the four highest GNP figures for the entire Soviet Union (the other being Russia). In September 1991, the Soviet Union recognised the independence of all three Baltic states, signalling the breakup of the Union itself. With a tradition of a well-educated workforce, offering low wage rates, the states immediately became the focus for foreign investment. While bringing new industry to the area, much of the wealth created rests in the headquarters of German and American transnational companies.

Without the central administration of Moscow, the Baltic states have had to develop government systems themselves. Energy prices rose dramatically, as supplies of cheap Soviet oil

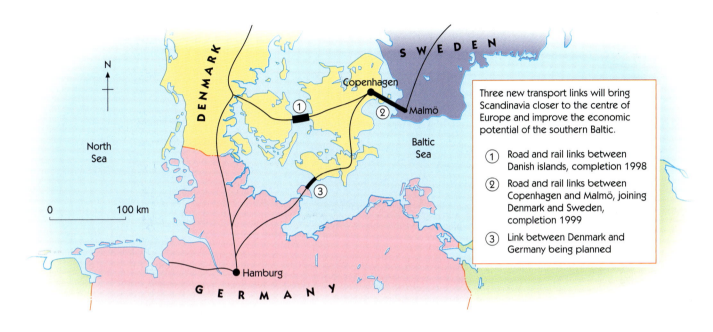

Figure E   The southern Baltic – growth area for the twenty-first century

Three new transport links will bring Scandinavia closer to the centre of Europe and improve the economic potential of the southern Baltic.

① Road and rail links between Danish islands, completion 1998

② Road and rail links between Copenhagen and Malmö, joining Denmark and Sweden, completion 1999

③ Link between Denmark and Germany being planned

and gas were withdrawn. GNP fell sharply as the change to a western style economy took place. Inflation rates in 1992 averaged over 1,000 % (see Figure F). Ethnic tensions remain throughout the Baltic states, where Russians make up 30 % of the population. In many ways, Lithuania, Estonia and Latvia remain in the vast shadow of Russia, ever conscious of the importance of their strategic and commercial location.

Since Finland and Sweden joined the EU in 1995 the economic potential of the Baltic region has increased. Helsinki, Stockholm and Copenhagen are all on the Baltic coast. Proposed transport links between Germany, Sweden and Denmark are likely to make the southern Baltic one of Europe's major economic growth areas in the twenty-first century. With a wealthy local market, skilled workforce and good transport and communications, the European core could extend north into Scandinavia in the near future (see pages 63–67).

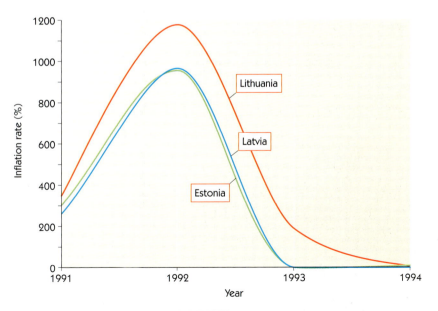

Figure F   Price inflation in the Baltic States

The Baltic – a polluted sea

The Baltic Sea (see Figure G) receives water from nearly 200 rivers, and is almost landlocked. Temperatures in the region are usually low, meaning that little water is evaporated. The result is that the Baltic is almost a freshwater sea. It is also very shallow, the average depth being only 50 metres. The Black Sea, by comparison, averages 1,271 metres.

The Baltic used to be famous for its stocks of fish, and the purity of its water. It has become the dumping ground for the industrial waste of countries bordering its shores. What is being done to solve the environmental problems of the Baltic Sea?

The Baltic region still contains much unspoiled landscape, and in many areas the population density is very low. Years of neglect have been replaced by an awareness of the environmental problems of the area. Yet, many problems remain. Co-operation between countries is sometimes difficult to achieve. The cost of pollution control is high, and more easily afforded by some countries than others. 'Green issues' may be important, but often take second place to the desire for economic growth and prosperity. The future of the Baltic Sea remains uncertain.

The problems

- The Soviet Union paid little attention to environmental protection.
- Many parts of the USSR were damaged by poorly planned industrial developments.
- In Estonia oil-shale mining caused severe pollution in the Baltic region and pumped dangerous ash into the atmosphere (see Figure H).
- Waste from the paper and plastics industries of Finland and Sweden have added to the problem.
- There are 300,000 tonnes of Second World War poisonous gas canisters dumped on the seabed.
- Sewage and fertilisers washed into rivers have concentrated in the Baltic Sea, leading to the rapid growth of algae, which suffocate marine life (**eutrophication**).
- The waters of the Baltic circulate very slowly, because of the narrow exits to the North Sea between Denmark and Sweden. This makes the build-up of algae a particular problem in the region.

The solutions

The problems of the Baltic Sea are international, and will only be solved by co-operation between the countries bordering the sea. The cost of cleaning up the environment is enormous, estimated to be as much as $20 billion. What has been done?

- The Helsinki Convention, involving all countries bordering the Baltic, recommended that member states should halve waste discharges into the Sea by 1995.
- The European Parliament has recommended that 1,200 new water treatment plants are needed in the region. The European Bank for Reconstruction and Development has given money to fund this development.
- There is increasing co-operation between countries. Finland, which blames Estonia for much of its acid rain, is helping to pay for the cost of cleaning up the pollution.
- Baltic governments, particularly in the post-communist states, are becoming more aware of 'green' issues. Organic farming is one example of how problems are being tackled.

Figure G The Baltic Sea

Figure H The burning of oil shale – one source of pollution in the Baltic

▼ Questions

1 Using a blank outline map of Europe, show the location of the countries which have recently applied to join the European Union. Use the map on page 5 to help you.

2 What do you think could be the advantages and disadvantages of a much bigger EU to:
   a present member states;
   b new members?

3 a List some of the political changes which have affected the Baltic region.
   b What are the main economic changes in the region? How do you see the Baltic developing in the twenty-first century?➡

4 There are concerns about the future of the North Sea (see pages 43–46), as there are with the Baltic. What are the main similarities between the problems faced by the two areas? How are they different?➡

Review

With the collapse of communism in eastern Europe, the influence of the European Union is set to extend across the continent. Several states have already applied to join the EU, with more likely to follow. The Baltic states of Lithuania, Estonia and Latvia, wealthy by the standards of the old Soviet Union, are struggling to adapt to changes since its breakup.

The Baltic is a potential European growth region for the twenty-first century. This is due to the expansion of the EU into Scandinavia, improving infrastructure, and the increasing prosperity of its people. The Baltic Sea has long been a dumping ground for many types of pollutants. The cleaning of the sea is a major task that will only be accomplished with international agreement.

4

Europe's population

Key ideas & questions

● The population of Europe is unevenly distributed. Some parts of western Europe are very densely populated.

● How is the structure of Europe's population changing? What is predicted to happen to population in the twenty-first century?

● Some European countries, for example Italy, are experiencing a decline in their population.

Main activity

Writing an article about Europe's population.

The population of Europe grew steadily from 1945–1985, then more slowly. The density of population is highest in western European countries. Until Austria, Finland and Sweden joined the European Union in 1995, the EU was one of the most densely populated regions in the world. The three new members, while occupying over one-quarter of its land area, are home to only 6 % of the Community's people.

Figure A The United Kingdom and Norway illustrate the great variety in Europe's population density

Europe's population is distributed unevenly across the continent (see page 8). Ireland and Finland, for example, have fewer than 50 people per square kilometre, while Belgium and the Netherlands exceed 300. Iceland, with only three people per square kilometre, is the most sparsely populated country in Europe.

These average figures mask enormous differences within countries. The most densely populated region of Europe is from north-west England to northern Italy, passing through parts of Belgium, the Netherlands and Germany. Compare this concentration of population with the European core area suggested on pages 63–67. The highest concentrations of people are usually in industrialised and urban areas. In Belgium, the Netherlands and the United Kingdom, for example, over 80 % of the population live in towns and cities. Sparsely populated regions are not always peripheral or poor areas. The Champagne region of northern France is an example of a wealthy area where population density is low, the economy being dominated by vast agricultural estates (see Figure B).

Do you know?

❓ Over 20 % of the European Union's people live on only 4 % of its land surface.

❓ Population increase in the European Union is less than 0.1 % per year, one of the slowest rates of growth in the world. Italy is declining with a 0.01 % natural loss per year.

❓ By the year 2020, it is predicted that over one-quarter of people living in the EU will be aged 60 years or over.

Figure B   The Champagne region of France

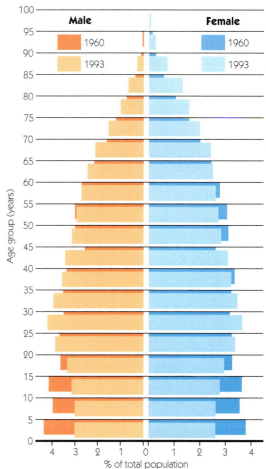

Figure C   Population change in the
European Union, 1960–1993

The population of the European Union is growing at a slower rate than the rest of the world. Between 1960 and 1995 the population of the EU grew by 17 %, during which time the population of Africa and South America doubled. In some countries, for example Italy and Germany, there has been a decline in population. This low rate of increase is due mainly to a fall in birth rate since the 1960s, leading to a lower number of young people (see Figure C).

Since the end of the Second World War, the European Union has gained population by migration. There are over 17 million foreign residents in EU countries, representing approximately 4.5 % of the total population. Many of these people live in Germany, France and the United Kingdom. Ireland is the only country in the European Union to experience an overall loss of population due to migration.

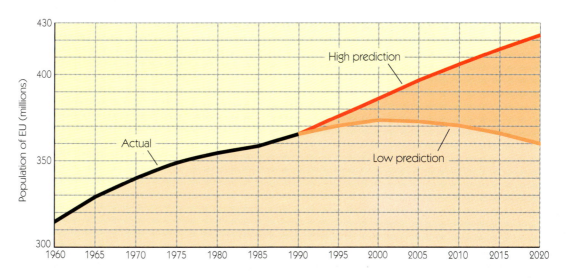

Figure D   Change in the population of the European Union

The future

Figure D predicts how Europe's population may change in the early years of the next century. Below there are two quite different estimates; one suggests a continued growth in population, the other a decline. The two forecasts are based upon the following assumptions:

1 The 'low' estimate

a That birth rates will continue to fall. For women born recently, the average number of children will be approximately 1.5.

b Life expectancy will continue to rise, but more slowly than at present in some parts of Europe, eventually levelling off next century.

c Migration levels into Europe will be reduced in the future.

2 The 'high' estimate

a Birth rates will begin to rise in the near future, reaching an average of two children per woman next century.

b Life expectancy will continue to rise substantially in the future.

c Migration into the EU will continue to increase.

One similarity between both predictions is the ageing of Europe's population. In addition to a falling birth rate, increasing life expectancy results in a greater proportion of the population being of retirement age (see Figure E). The population of all countries in the European Union is ageing, although the trend is most noticeable in Italy, Belgium and the United Kingdom. Recent reduction in the birth rates of Ireland, Greece and Portugal will soon lead to a similar pattern arising in these countries. An ageing population poses many problems, for example, the funding of pensions and other payments by a smaller proportion of people who are in employment. Population ageing is a global trend, which will eventually affect economically developing countries.

Population of the EU by age group (%)

	0–19	20–50	60+
1960	31.8	52.8	15.4
1965	32.3	51.4	16.4
1970	32.1	50.4	17.5
1975	31.5	50.3	18.2
1980	30.1	52.0	17.9
1985	27.8	53.4	18.8
1990	25.5	54.9	19.6
1995	24.2	55.4	20.4
2000	23.8	55.0	21.3
2005	23.4	54.6	22.0
2010	22.9	53.9	23.2
2015	22.2	53.5	24.3
2020	21.6	52.8	25.7

☐ Predictions

Figure E   The European Union's ageing population

▼ Questions

1 Describe the main differences in the distribution of Europe's population.

2 What do you think are the main reasons for these differences? You might find it useful to refer to the maps on pages 5–8, and an atlas to help you with your answer.

3 Write an article about Europe's population. You will need to use information from this chapter, an atlas and other sources. Here is a checklist for your article:➡

a Total EU and European population.
b Distribution and density.
c Birth rates, death rates and natural change.
d Migration within Europe.
e Migration into Europe.
f Other features,
   e.g. life expectancy;   infant mortality;
         age-sex pyramids;   ageing populations.

Use headlines and sub-headings.
Use a country of your own choice as a case study.

Review

The population of Europe is unevenly distributed. Much of western Europe is very densely inhabited, and highly urbanised. The greatest concentration of people extends from northern England to the north of Italy. Europe's population is growing at a slower rate than other parts of the world, due mainly to a decrease in birth rates. This is leading to an ageing population. Estimates for future increases in population vary, with the possibility of a decline in the next century. Some countries, for example Italy, are currently experiencing a fall in their population.

Key ideas & questions

● The structure and function of cities change continually.

● The role of planning is essential for the future growth of urban areas.

● How has Berlin been affected by its division after the Second World War?

● How are Berlin's planners trying to solve the city's problems?

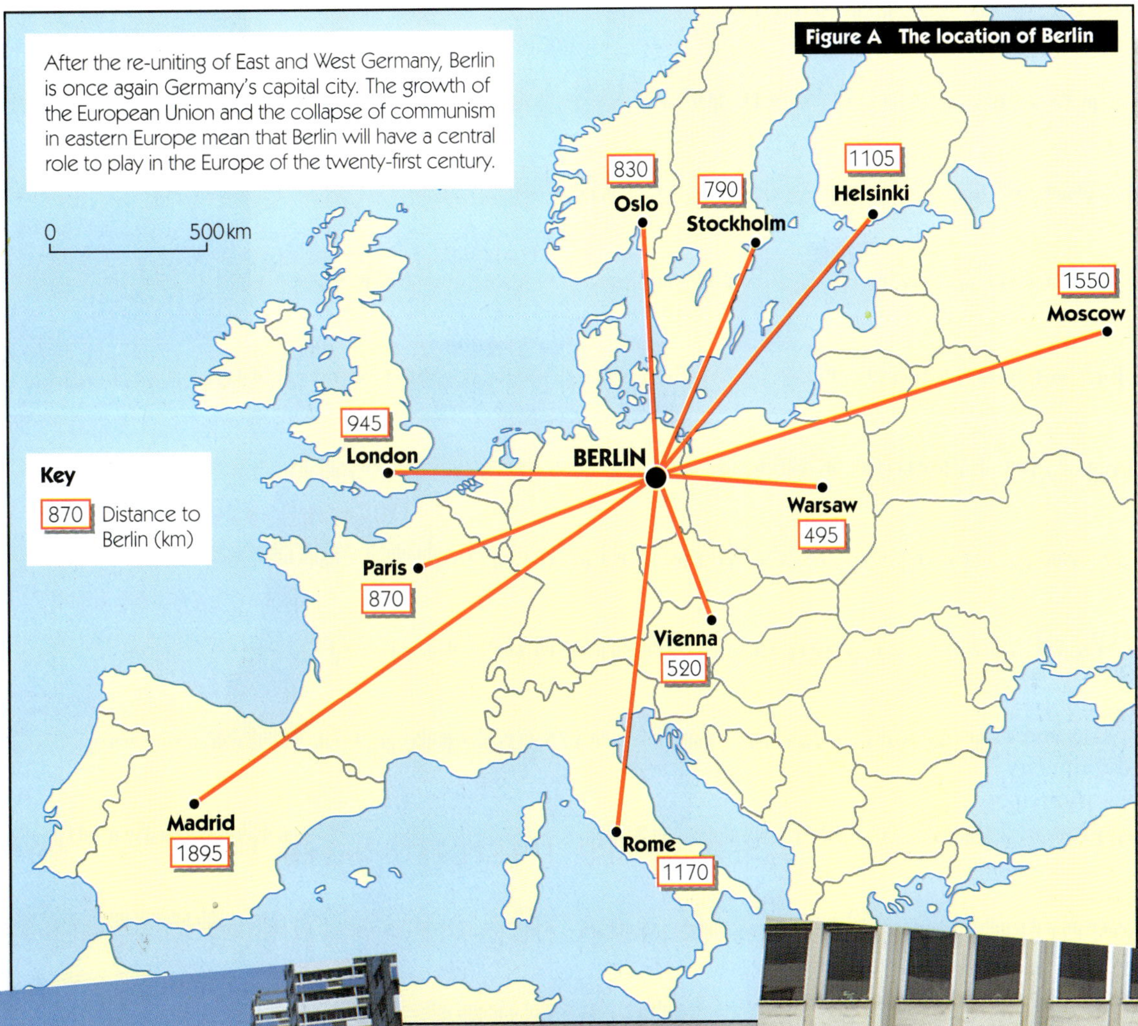

Do you know?

? Berlin lies on the North German Plain, at the meeting point of several rivers and amid many lakes.

? The river Spree is connected by waterways to the Baltic Sea.

? Over 100 people were shot dead attempting to cross the Berlin Wall into West Berlin between 1961 and 1989.

Main activity

An annotated sketch map, suitable for use in a GCSE examination answer, together with background questions on Berlin.

Berlin is Germany's largest city with a population of nearly 3.5 million people. It is also one of the country's 16 regional States. The Berlin Region, consisting of eight urban and rural areas surrounding the city, houses another million people. The area forms the second largest conurbation in Germany, behind the Rhine–Ruhr region with a population of 12 million. It is estimated that the population of Greater Berlin will increase by about one million within the next 15 years, about a third of which will be in the city itself.

Figure A   The location of Berlin

After the re-uniting of East and West Germany, Berlin is once again Germany's capital city. The growth of the European Union and the collapse of communism in eastern Europe mean that Berlin will have a central role to play in the Europe of the twenty-first century.

0   500 km

Oslo 830
Stockholm 790
Helsinki 1105
Moscow 1550
London 945
BERLIN
Warsaw 495
Paris 870
Vienna 520
Madrid 1895
Rome 1170

Key
870 Distance to Berlin (km)

Figure B   Pre-fabricated tower blocks from the 1970s in the eastern part of Berlin

Figure C   Before becoming united as one city again in 1989, the west of Berlin contained the bulk of the city's population and wealth

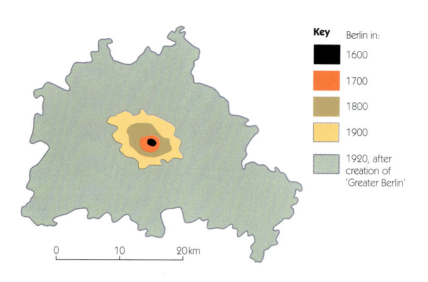

Key Berlin in:

- ■ 1600
- ■ 1700
- ■ 1800
- ■ 1900
- ■ 1920, after creation of 'Greater Berlin'

0   10   20 km

Figure D The growth of Berlin

Figure E   The Berlin Wall divided the city for nearly 30 years

Berlin's recent history has provided unique problems for planners. At the beginning of the twentieth century, Berlin had grown to a city with 1,888,000 inhabitants. In 1920, following the First World War, the city boundaries expanded to include surrounding towns and villages (see Figure D). The population of the new Greater Berlin was nearly four million people.

The end of the Second World War saw the city divided among the victorious powers of Britain, France, the USA and the Soviet Union. The city had been devastated by the War. Over 600,000 apartments, the main type of private dwelling in Berlin, had been destroyed. The pre-war population of 4.3 million stood at only 2.8 million. Most of the city's infrastructure was in ruins.

In 1948 the Soviet Union tried to cut the city off in order to force the other countries to pull out of Berlin and leave it under Russian control. The attempt failed, but in 1949 East Berlin, controlled by the Russians, became capital of the newly created East Germany. In the 1950s the three western sectors and East Berlin grew more and more apart. The city's partition seemed to be cemented for ever when, in 1961,

1 Building and housing

Most of Berlin's 1.8 million dwellings are rented. Only 9 % are owner-occupied, and the German government predicts that the city faces a housing crisis in the near future. Research estimates that 150,000 more flats (the main type of residence in Berlin) will be needed by the end of the century. This is because of the rapid increase in the city's population, and the fact that more and more people want their own flat. One household in two in Berlin consists of only one person.

Approximately one-third of the population growth in Greater Berlin is likely to be within the city itself. The focus for building is to expand and develop existing residential areas, while preserving the relatively low densities of much of the city. Woodland accounts for 24 % of Berlin, and the authorities plan 16 new parks to help preserve the city's 'green' status. Large building projects extending the city northwards are also designed to take pressure off the housing market (see Figure F).

The majority of population growth is predicted to take place in the city's hinterland, expanding into the surrounding region of Brandenburg. A series of regional development centres are planned. These will be linked to each other, and to Berlin, by fast rail systems.

the East Germans built the Berlin Wall in order to stop the steady flow of migrants into West Berlin (see Figure E). East and West Berlin developed completely separately, with hardly any official contact between the two.

Until the demolition of the Wall in 1989, the two halves of the city grew independently of each other. Both East and West Berlin set out urban plans in the 1980s which related only to their part of the city. The geography of Berlin changed dramatically after Germany became one country, and as the city once more became the nation's capital. A barren strip of land, up to 200 metres in width, which was left over from the Berlin Wall, cut right through the middle of the city.

In 1994 the first plan for the whole of Berlin focused on two main problems as priorities.
1 New building was urgently required, particularly housing to cope with Berlin's growing population.
2 The city's transport systems had to be improved, especially with Berlin resuming its function as the nation's capital city.

Figure F   A ring of developments in and around Berlin will supply most of the housing needs of the growing city

Despite these efforts, there is still likely to be a shortage of housing in Berlin in the future. In addition to new buildings, the city has to cope with the cost of renovating the prefabricated flats in former East Berlin, many of which are in poor condition. Government funds are limited, and Berlin urgently requires greater private investment to solve its housing problem.

2 Transport

Before the Second World War Berlin had a fully developed modern transport system, its backbone consisting of 300 kilometres of inner city railway lines. Berlin had Europe's second largest inland port, and Templehof airport was one of the most important in the world.

After reunification, it was not possible simply to restore these facilities. War damage had been poorly restored and the transport system had developed separately to meet the demand on each side of the city after the Wall was built. The German government is now investing heavily in public transport to meet the needs of Berlin's growing population.

The re-development of Berlin's transport system centres on the provision of public transport. It is intended that only 20 % of transport into the city centre should be private. The reconnected system of trams, buses and underground railways already carry over a billion passengers each year. Berlin's new railway system will link with the areas of urban development beyond the city and elsewhere in Germany (see Figure G).

Within the city an 800 kilometre network of pathways encourages commuters to cycle to and from the city centre. Transport along Berlin's waterways is also likely to increase in the future. A new airport, to the south of Berlin, Berlin-Brandenburg International, is planned by the year 2010.

Figure H   The city's transport system is designed to encourage people away from their cars

Key

- U-Bahn network (existing)
- U-Bahn (planned)
- S-Bahn network (existing)
- S-Bahn network (planned)
- Major terminals

Main transfer stations

1. Westkreuz
2. Zoo
3. Lehrter Bahnhof
4. Friedrichstrasse
5. Alexanderplatz
6. Ostkreuz

Oranienburg • Bernau • Ahrensfelde • Wartenberg • Nauen • Strausberg • Wannsee • Spindlersfeld • Lichterfelde Süd • Ekner • Potsdam • Blankenfelde • Schönefeld • Königs Wusterhausen

0   10   20km

Figure G   Existing and planned rail networks in Berlin

Berlin–Brandenburg

Berlin is surrounded by the region of Brandenburg (see Figure I). Since the reunification of Germany, the government has been planning to join the capital city and surrounding state into one region by the start of the next century. The new region of Berlin–Brandenburg would have a population of over six million, in an area about the same size as North Rhine-Westphalia. It would become the fifth largest region in Germany and one of Europe's biggest economic regions. Close links already exist between the two states, with Brandenburg being an important commuter zone for Berlin.

Berlin is still coming to terms with the problems caused by its divided history. Isolated from the rest of the former West Germany, West Berlin kept pace with the rest of the country through massive grants from the government. After reunification, the difference in living standards between the two halves of the city was stark. The most pressing problem for the city remains to bridge the gap in living standards and quality of life between east and west.

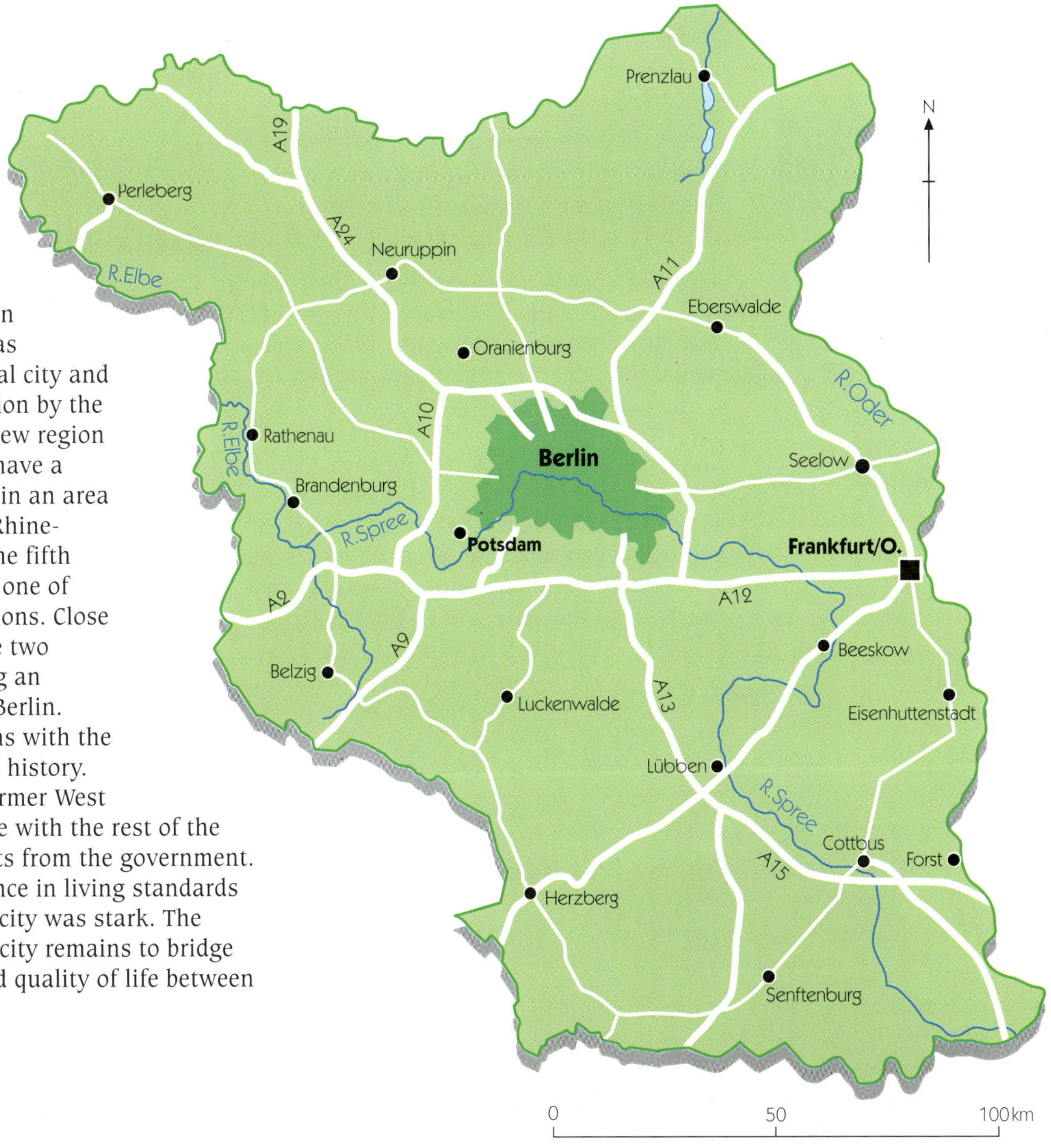

Figure I Berlin–Brandenburg

▼ Questions

1 Describe how Berlin's population has changed since 1920 to the present day.

2 What were the main effects on the city of its division after the Second World War?

3 How have planners attempted to solve the problems facing Berlin? ➡

4 Sketch maps are an important part of many exam papers. A good sketch map can be a valuable revision aid, as well as part of an examination answer. Most Named Examples may be illustrated through the use of a sketch map. For a sketch map, you should:

   a Draw a base map, showing the general location of the case study.

   b Add any relevant physical or natural features e.g. rivers, relief.

   c Add human and economic features to your map.

In each case, the features should be annotated, i.e. with an accurately located label giving relevant details.

Using the outline above, draw a sketch map to show the important features of the case study on Berlin.

Review

Berlin is the largest city in Germany. The city's hinterland, including the state of Brandenburg, contains over six million people. After the Second World War, the city was divided into East and West Berlin, with the Berlin Wall being built in 1961 to separate the two. The Wall was demolished in 1989 and Berlin, like Germany, became reunited.

The separate development of the years after the War have left Berlin with many problems. The east of the city, under communist rule, was much poorer than the west. Transport systems have had to be redesigned and much rebuilding has taken place. The city has once again become the German capital, and is an area of rapid growth that is likely to play an important role in the development of Europe in the twenty-first century.

CASE STUDY: Population change in Germany

Key ideas & questions

● Birth rates and migration affect population structure and change.
● How have migration and the reuniting of Germany affected the country's population structure?

Main activity

This is a GCSE examination-style question highlighting the importance of case studies.

Germany has a population of 82 million people, including 7.2 million foreigners. It is one of the most densely populated countries in Europe, behind Belgium, the Netherlands and the UK.

The population of Germany is distributed very unevenly (see Figure A). The Berlin region, which has been growing rapidly since East and West Germany reunited, has a population of 4.5 million. This is forecast to increase to 5.5 million by the year 2000. More than 11 million people live in the Rhine–Ruhr industrial area, where towns and cities are so close together that there are no distinct boundaries between them. Densely populated regions contrast with very sparsely populated regions such as the moorlands of the North German Plain and the Bavarian Mountains. The area of former West Germany is much more heavily populated than the East, where less than one-fifth of the population live on 30 % of the national territory. Of the 13 cities with more than 500,000 inhabitants, only two are in the eastern part of Germany (see Figure C). Although one-third of the German population live in cities with more than 100,000 inhabitants, the majority of people live in small towns and villages.

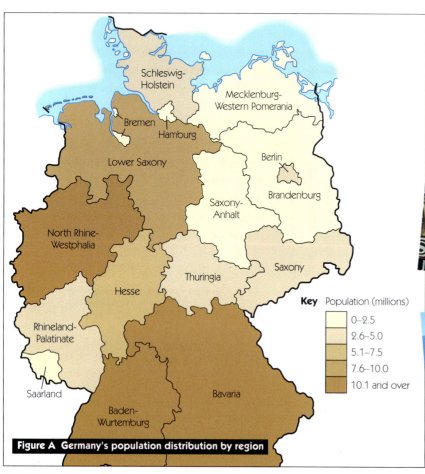

Figure A Germany's population distribution by region

Key Population (millions)

	0–2.5
	2.6–5.0
	5.1–7.5
	7.6–10.0
	10.1 and over

Regions labelled on map: Schleswig-Holstein, Mecklenburg-Western Pomerania, Bremen, Hamburg, Lower Saxony, Berlin, Brandenburg, Saxony-Anhalt, North Rhine-Westphalia, Thuringia, Saxony, Hesse, Rhineland-Palatinate, Saarland, Baden-Wurtemburg, Bavaria

Figure B   Munich – a densely populated area of Germany

Lower Saxony – a sparsely-populated area

Do you know?

? Agriculture plays a relatively unimportant part in Germany's economy and the country imports about one-third of its food.
? The dominance of manufacturing industries has serious effects on the environment. Germany faces many air and water pollution problems.
? Germany is Europe's leading consumer of coal and oil, although the country's consumption of coal has halved since 1989.

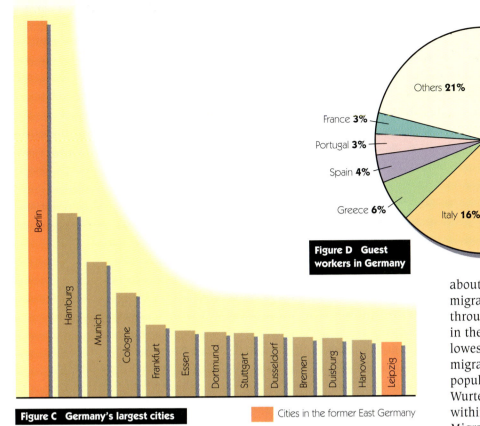

Figure D Guest workers in Germany

Others **21%**
France **3%**
Portugal **3%**
Spain **4%**
Greece **6%**
Italy **16%**
Yugoslavia **17%**
Turkey **30%**

Figure C Germany's largest cities

Berlin, Hamburg, Munich, Cologne, Frankfurt, Essen, Dortmund, Stuttgart, Dusseldorf, Bremen, Duisburg, Hanover, Leipzig

■ Cities in the former East Germany

Population change

Population increased in Germany after the Second World War due mainly to immigration. About 13 million refugees entered the present German territory from the former German eastern provinces and eastern Europe. There was a continuous flow of people from East to West Germany until the border was closed and the Berlin Wall was erected in 1961. Migrants came from poorer southern and eastern European countries to occupy low paid jobs in the country's expanding economy. By 1990, these 'guest workers' accounted for over 7 % of West Germany's workforce (see Figure D).

The 1990s has seen changes to the structure of the German population, brought about both by natural increase and by migration. Population began to decline throughout Germany by the 1970s due to a fall in the birth rate. Germany still has one of the lowest birth rates in the world. Since 1990 migration has led to a slight increase in population. Hamburg, Bremen and Baden Wurtemburg have the highest rates of migration within Germany, slightly over 2 % per year. Migrants now come into Germany from a growing list of countries (see Figure E). This is due mainly to increased integration within the European Union and the western world, and the collapse of communist eastern European governments. While the highest number of migrants (over 2,000,000) are from Turkey, people have moved to Germany from as far afield as Vietnam, Iran and Brazil.

The overwhelming majority of foreigners live in the western part of the country, with more than half having lived in Germany for ten years or more. The German government aims to integrate foreign workers and their families into German society, and is committed to the strict limitation of further immigration from countries outside the European Union. Increased unemployment leading to attacks on non-German groups has made integration difficult. With such a low birth rate, the future growth and structure of the German population is likely to depend upon the government's policy on accepting migrants into the country.

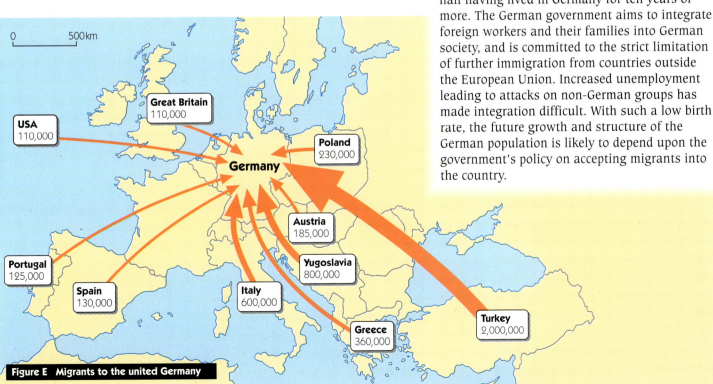

0   500km

USA 110,000
Great Britain 110,000
Poland 230,000
Germany
Austria 185,000
Portugal 125,000
Spain 130,000
Italy 600,000
Yugoslavia 800,000
Greece 360,000
Turkey 2,000,000

Figure E Migrants to the united Germany

Germany reunited

At the end of the Second World War, a defeated Germany became divided among the victorious powers of Britain, France, the USA and the Soviet Union. Although originally intended to be a temporary split, by 1949 both East and West Germany had formally been established. The West, with three-quarters of the population, rebuilt war damage and prospered. Sustained growth saw the country become the world's third largest economy, and its leading exporter. The East was to be the industrial showpiece of the Soviet European empire. By the late 1980s it was clear that the Soviet empire was crumbling. The supposed economic miracle had not happened, and East Germans were leaving the country by all means possible. A year after the collapse of the East German government in 1989, the country was officially united.

Figure F After nearly half a decade as a divided city, Berlin is building again as Germany's capital city

Like defeated Germany itself, the pre-war capital Berlin had been divided. The Berlin Wall isolated West Berliners 100 miles within East Germany. When East Germany joined the West, it was agreed that Berlin would become the official capital of Germany.

The costs of reunification have been high. Although the most prosperous country within the Soviet empire, East Germany was significantly poorer than advanced EU countries. Massive investment was required to restore industry and transport in the East, meaning increased taxes for all Germans. Germany became a major donor of aid to eastern Europe and to former Soviet republics. The German economy suffered as the 1990s saw a decline in world trade which hit the country's exports.

There have been social as well as economic effects of reunification. West Germans resented added taxes and the cost of reunification. Unrest resulted in a series of strikes and demonstrations, unheard of in recent German history. Easterners objected to the control and domination of the West. At the very least, reuniting Germany is likely to be a more lengthy process than anybody thought when the Berlin Wall was destroyed.

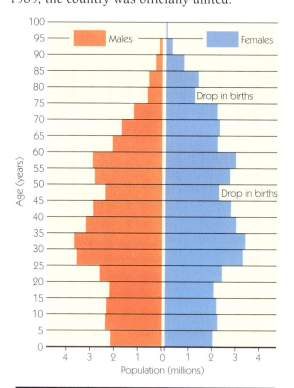
Figure G Age/sex structure of the German population, 1995

Review

Germany, like many other European countries, has a very unevenly distributed population. The area of the former West Germany is more heavily populated than the area that was East Germany. After the Second World War, West Germany's population was increased by migration; as a consequence, the migrant population is highest in the west of reunited Germany. Since reunification, the difference in wealth between the two former parts of Germany has caused many problems, some of which have yet to be solved.

▼ Questions

The questions below are typical of the type set for higher tier GCSE Geography examinations. As a practice question, you should spend 25 minutes in total. Places and Cases will help you with the Named Example and with the maps on pages 5–8, but you may have to refer to a core text for help with other parts of the question.

1 What is meant by the term migration?   (1 mark)
2 What are the main reasons for an economically developed country receiving migrants?   (3 marks)
3 What problems could face an economically developed country receiving large numbers of migrants?   (3 marks)

Figure G shows the age structure of the German population. Use the diagram to answer the following questions.

4 Describe the structure of the population under each of the following headings:

a dependants (under 16)
b working age (17–65)
c retirement (66 and over)
                                      (3 marks)
d Why do you think there is a drop in births in the places shown on the diagram?
                                      (2 marks)
e Compare and contrast the structure of the diagram for Germany with that of a named economically developing country.   (5 marks)
5 Figure E shows the origin of migrants to Germany. Describe and explain the pattern of migrants shown on the map.
                                      (5 marks)
6 Named example:
For an EU country that you have studied, explain the regional variations in population distribution.
                                      (8 marks)

Total 30 marks

Migration

Key ideas & questions

● People move because of a variety of push and pull factors.
● Migration has effects both on the areas people have left, and on the areas to which they move.
● What effects has migration had on the structure and distribution of population in France?

Main activity

Analysing migration and discussing its effects.

Do you know?

? Migration has always been an important part of Europe's changing population.
? Most of the migrant population from outside the EU lives in three countries. These are Germany, France and the United Kingdom.
? The large number of migrants in the European Union can be explained by immigration in response to the need for labour, particularly low paid jobs, and by the appeal of the European Union to people in non-member countries.

Figure A   Algeria, a developing country. Population has increased by 40 % in the last 15 years.

Italy's population growth during the same period was little over 1 %. This is typical of many developed countries.

A global migration problem?

As a result of poverty, drought and conflict, millions of people within developing countries are forced to leave their homes. Although a substantial portion of this movement takes place within poorer countries, in the last 40 years about 35 million people have migrated to rich industrialised nations (about six million illegally). The enormous difference in wealth between rich and poor nations has contributed to the flow of migrants from developing countries. The poorest 20 % of the world's population earn only 1.4 % of world GNP, while the richest 20 % share nearly 83 %.

It is estimated that by 2025 the population of the world will be 8.5 billion, compared with just over 5 billion in 1990. Most of this growth is likely to occur in the developing countries. The European Union will have only about 4 % of the world's population, compared with 6.5 % at present (see Figure B). With such little growth, the EU will have an increasingly ageing population. Within the next 25 years, it is predicted that nearly 30 % of Europeans will be over the age of 60. With a decline in the number of people of working age, the nations of Europe could need more workers from abroad to maintain economic prosperity, increasing migration into the continent.

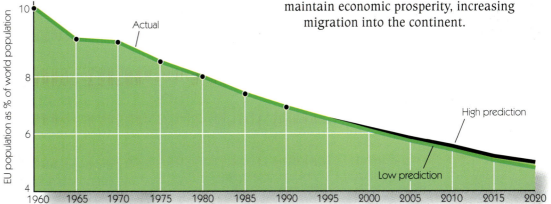

Figure B   EU population as a percentage of world population

CASE STUDY: Migration into France

The population of France, 54 million, is nearly the same as the United Kingdom. Average population density, however, is much lower as France is a larger country (102 people per square kilometre in France compared with 238 in the United Kingdom). There are great regional variations in the distribution of France's population (see Figure C). The largest cities (Paris, Lyon and Marseilles) are all centres of regions of high population density, along with established industrial areas such as Lille. Seventy-four per cent of France's population is concentrated in urban areas, with the result that large areas of the country are sparsely populated (see Figure D). The central region of Limousin has only 50 people per square kilometre, compared with

Figure D Paris and Ille-de France region is the most densely populated part of France

Much of France is sparsely populated

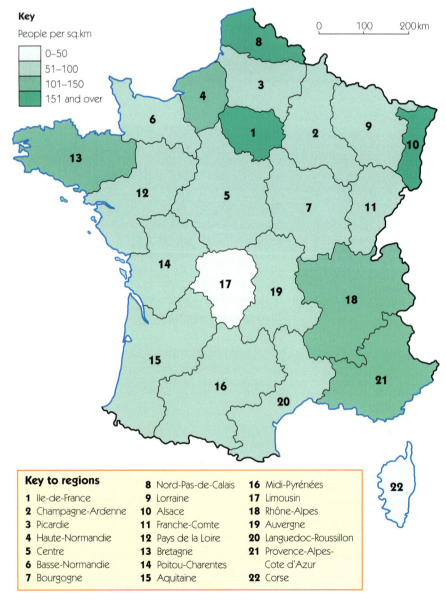

Key

People per sq.km

- 0–50
- 51–100
- 101–150
- 151 and over

0   100   200 km

Key to regions

1 Ile-de-France	8 Nord-Pas-de-Calais	16 Midi-Pyrénées
2 Champagne-Ardenne	9 Lorraine	17 Limousin
3 Picardie	10 Alsace	18 Rhône-Alpes
4 Haute-Normandie	11 Franche-Comte	19 Auvergne
5 Centre	12 Pays de la Loire	20 Languedoc-Roussillon
6 Basse-Normandie	13 Bretagne	21 Provence-Alpes-
7 Bourgogne	14 Poitou-Charentes	Cote d'Azur
	15 Aquitaine	22 Corse

Figure C   The regional population distribution of France

nearly 900 in the Ille-de-France region around Paris where one-fifth of the French population live.

Most regions of France have experienced significant changes in population in recent years. Along with other western European countries, France has a low birth rate and high life expectancy, resulting in an ageing population. Population change is also caused by migration, both within France and from other countries.

Migration within France, shown in Figure E, is a response to changes in employment structure within the country. There has been a steady decline in primary industry, from 16 % of the working population in 1970 to only 4 % at present. As a result, the movement of people away from some of France's main agricultural regions has countered any natural increase in the population. The centre and north-west of the country has been affected most by this decline.

The most significant migration within France has been away from the traditional heavy industrial areas of the north-east of the country. Lorraine and Nord-Pas-de-Calais have

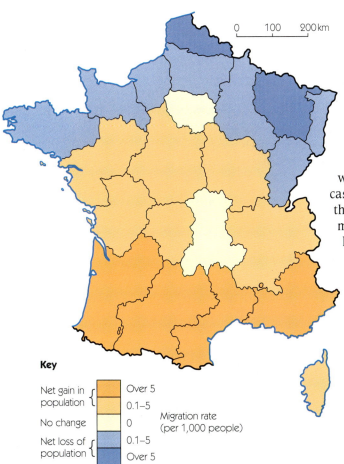

Key

Net gain in population {	Over 5	
	0.1–5	
No change	0	Migration rate (per 1,000 people)
Net loss of population {	0.1–5	
	Over 5	

Figure E   Migration – population gains and losses in France

experienced the greatest loss due to the decline in employment in industry. Although employment in manufacturing industry has declined throughout France, this has been least noticeable in the regions in the south of the country.

It is to these Mediterranean regions, where most new jobs have been located, that the greatest migration has taken place. In addition to hi-tech industries, tourism has given a major boost to the economy of southern France.

After Germany, France has the largest number of foreign residents within the European Union (see Figure F). France suffered heavy casualties during the First World War, causing a serious decline in the population. The country became home to migrant workers from many nations in order to help fill the resulting labour shortage. The largest numbers came initially from Italy and Poland, and then from Spain as a result of the Spanish Civil War.

Following the Second World War, migrant numbers increased, particularly following the end of colonial rule by European countries (see Figure G). People fled Africa due to the political instability which often followed independence from colonial occupation, as well as the fear of wars or ethnic cleansing. Migrants came to France from north Africa, notably

Number of migrants (in millions) into the 3 major EU countries (75% of total migrants)

4.2 Germany

2.3 France

1.2 United Kingdom

Figure F   75 % of migrants into the European Union live in three countries

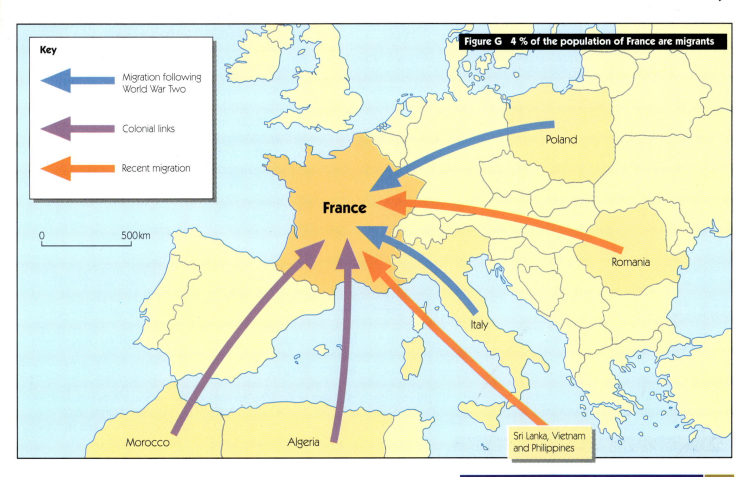

Key

Migration following World War Two

Colonial links

Recent migration

Figure G   4 % of the population of France are migrants

France

Poland

Romania

Italy

Morocco

Algeria

Sri Lanka, Vietnam and Philippines

Algeria and Morocco. Initial migrants would often be male, seeking jobs in Europe to send money back home. After becoming full residents of France, the workers would then be joined by their families. This meant that the migrant population of France was young, often with a majority of males.

Migration has been greatest into the south and east of France, for example in the region around Marseilles. The expansion of the French colonies in Africa made Marseilles an important link between the two continents. The continued expansion of the city into Europe's second largest port led to a large influx of African workers. Today, about 10 % of the population of Marseilles is of African origin, mostly from Algeria.

More recently France has attracted migrants from Asia (namely Sri Lanka, the Philippines and Vietnam), and central and eastern Europe, along with other members of the European Union. What has made migration into a possible crisis and therefore an important political issue is the number of people who have entered France illegally. Although migration has been mainly from African and other developing countries, the problem has been made worse since 1990 by the flow of refugees from countries like Romania and the former Yugoslavia.

Since 1994 the French authorities have taken measures to restrict illegal immigration and to control the entry of refugees into the country. In addition, it has become more difficult for legal migrants to become French citizens, especially those from Arab or Islamic countries. Before, migrants could readily obtain French citizenship, which also applied to any of their children born in France. Today, government policies have made it harder for migrants to gain work permits, or for workers to be joined in France by other members of their family.

The movement of people into France continues to have a major impact upon population structures. An estimated 4 % of the population of France are migrants; 2 % are Muslim, mostly from Algeria, Morocco and Tunisia. Over one million French people are descendants of north African migrant labourers, many of whom are aged 25 or under. About 14 million people, or a quarter of the total population of France, have a parent or grandparent who was a migrant into the country.

Figure H   Migrants have been attracted to Nanterre, a town outside Paris

France faces a dilemma over migration in the near future. The government has tried to control immigration, particularly the flow of illegal migrants and refugees. However, the nature of the country's ageing population means that France is likely to face a labour shortage early in the twenty-first century. Government estimates suggest that France will need about 150,000 extra workers each year in order to meet this shortage, which has traditionally been met with workers from abroad.

▼ Questions

1 Which European Union countries receive the most migrants?

2 Migrants may be 'pushed' away from their home area, or they may be 'pulled' to the area to which they move. For migrants into EU countries, make a list of possible push and pull factors.

3 Describe and explain migration in France under the following headings:
   a Migration within France.
   b Migration into France.

4 What role do you think migration will play in the population structure of Europe in the twenty-first century? Give reasons for your answer.

Review

Migration has always been an important part of the changing population structure of Europe. Relatively high levels of income, particularly in western Europe, make the European Union an attractive destination for migrants. Many migrants have moved to Europe in response to labour shortages, but generally occupy low paid jobs.

France has the second highest number of migrants in Europe, behind Germany. Many of these have moved from north Africa since the Second World War, although migrants to France also come from Asia and eastern Europe. The highest concentrations of migrants in France are in the south and east of the country. France is trying to control the number of people moving into the country, but faces a possible labour shortage in the near future.

5

Europe and the wider world

Do you know?

? **International trade** is the exchange of goods, commodities and services between countries.

? Trade involving goods and commodities is called **visible trade**. Trade involving services is called **invisible trade**.

? The total value of a country's imports compared to its exports is called the **balance of trade**.

? If a country earns more from exports than the cost of its imports, it is said to have a **trade surplus**.

? If the cost of imports exceeds the value of exports, a country has a **trade deficit**.

Main activity

A comparison of the levels of development aid provided by different European countries.

The European Union is the world's leading trading power. In 1994 the EU accounted for over 20 % of world trade, compared with 18 % for the USA and 10 % for Japan. This only takes into account trade with countries outside the Union. Trade within the European Union has increased significantly, particularly since the establishment of a single market for trading. Over half of the EU's trade is now between member states.

The majority of the European Union's international trade is with industrialised countries, notably Japan and the USA. This consists mainly of manufactured goods, for example, motor vehicles and electrical machinery. Despite an overall growth in exports, the EU still relies heavily upon imports from other industrialised countries, particularly Japan (see Figure B). Trade between EU countries and eastern Europe has increased dramatically since the breakdown of the political and trading structures imposed by communism. Since 1990 trading agreements

introduced by the EU have encouraged links with eastern Europe and Russia.

The European Union's trade with economically developing countries is linked to the world distribution of natural resources. Petroleum products, for example, represent nearly a quarter of the EU's imports from the developing countries (see Figure D). On the other hand, the majority of the EU's exports to these developing countries consist of manufactured goods. As with its trade in eastern Europe, the European Union has a trade surplus with developing countries (see Figure C).

Figure B The greatest value of goods imported into the EU is from Japan

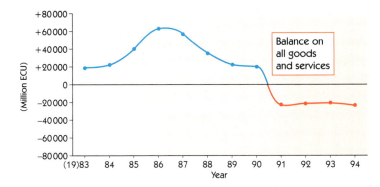

Figure A The EU operates an overall trading defect, importing more than it exports

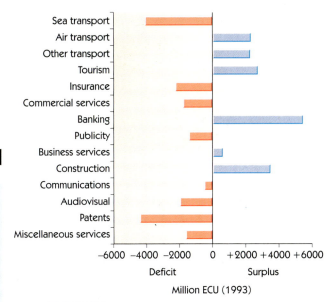

Figure C

Key ideas & questions

● International trade is an essential feature of most industries. The nature of the trade varies between countries of different economic standing.
● What is the pattern of the European Union's international trade?
● In what ways does the European Union provide development aid for poorer countries?
● How does Sweden contribute to international development aid?

Figure D Europe still relies upon imports of oil. The Middle East dominates production, with an estimated two thirds of world reserves.

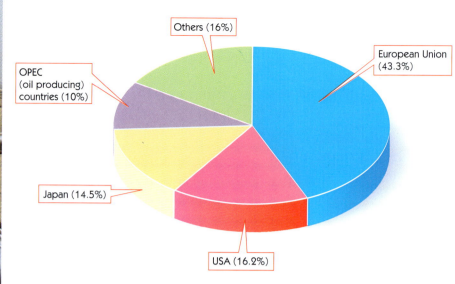

Others (16%)

European Union (43.3%)

OPEC (oil producing) countries (10%)

Japan (14.5%)

USA (16.2%)

Figure E   The European Union's contribution to overseas development aid

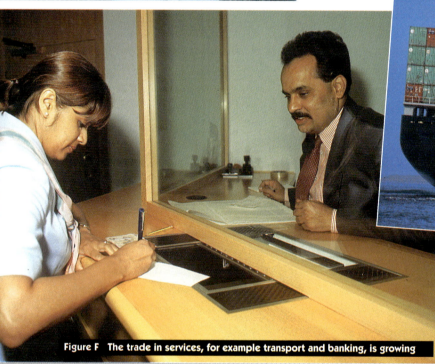

Figure F   The trade in services, for example transport and banking, is growing

An important growth area is the trade in service industries (or invisible trade) which account for about one third of EU trade. The United States is responsible for 30 % of this trade, which includes industries such as tourism, banking and insurance (see Figure F). There is currently a trade deficit with the EU's invisible trade, due largely to the phenomenal growth and dominance of these industries in the USA.

Aid and Development

Western industrialised nations provide aid for economically developing countries. This may be in the form of money or resources, for example manufactured goods or technical expertise. The European Union is the most important donor of aid in the world, contributing nearly one half of official or world government aid (see Figure E). Developing countries also receive voluntary aid, from organisations such as Oxfam and Christian Aid. There are also many trade agreements between individual countries. In some cases particular goods may be traded directly for specific products.

In principle, aid to developing countries should encourage sustainable development, and put the needs of people first. The benefits of overseas aid include the development of education and health care services and the expansion of industry, enabling less reliance on expensive imports.

In practice, aid can cause as many problems as it solves. It is often the urban and wealthy of a recipient country who benefit, rather than the rural poor in the greatest need. Aid may be used to exert political pressure upon a country, and could increase the long-term dependence of poorer countries. In recent years, many industrialised countries have gone through a period of economic recession. In such times, there is pressure upon governments to help people living in the donor countries rather than send money abroad.

The European Union provides development aid to countries totalling 80 % of the world's population. This includes the countries of central and eastern Europe, lagging behind the rest of the continent after decades of communist rule. The largest EU contribution is to the countries of Africa, the Caribbean and the Pacific (ACP countries, see Figure G), where the quantity of aid donated has increased dramatically since the early years of the Union. The Lomé Convention (see below) means that the European Union encourages trade with and provides aid for these countries, as with other developing nations.

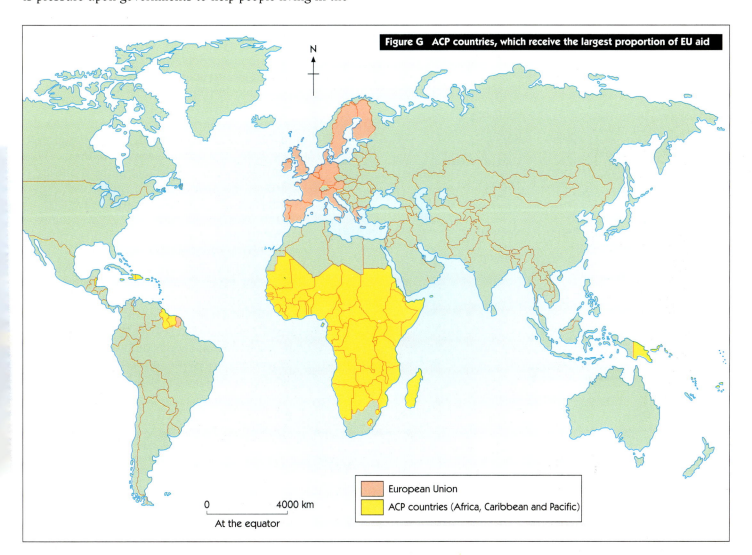

Figure G   ACP countries, which receive the largest proportion of EU aid

N

0 ———— 4000 km
At the equator

■ European Union
■ ACP countries (Africa, Caribbean and Pacific)

The Lomé Convention

The Lomé Convention, named after the city in Togo, West Africa, where it was signed, is at the centre of the European Union's aid and development policy. The convention gives trade concessions, credits and grants to 70 African, Caribbean and Pacific nations.

In addition to regional development activities, the EU is also involved in food aid programmes.

The Union is committed to providing over 1.5 million tonnes of grain to developing countries every year. In terms of total government aid, France and Germany contribute the greatest amounts. Figure H shows some of the major donors of development aid. Notice the difference between the two sets of figures. Which do you think gives a more accurate measure of the amount of aid a country is giving, or should give?

Sweden, one of the wealthiest countries in Europe, has been contributing to international development programmes for nearly 50 years. The Swedish government is committed to giving 1.0 % of its GNP for development aid. Currently, the actual amount of official aid donated is approximately 0.9 % of the country's wealth, which compares favourably with other European countries (see Figure H).

Overseas development aid

	% of GNP		in $ billion
Denmark	1.03	France	7.90
Norway	1.01	Germany	6.85
The Netherlands	0.81	Italy	2.91
France	0.63	United Kingdom	2.89
Finland	0.46	The Netherlands	2.52
Belgium	0.39	Denmark	1.33
Germany	0.36	Norway	1.01
Luxembourg	0.32	Finland	0.36
United Kingdom	0.31	Ireland	0.08
Italy	0.30	Luxembourg	0.05
Ireland	0.19		

Figure H   Development aid contributions

Over two thirds of the assistance is given as **bilateral aid**. This means that it is allocated to a specific country, for example disaster relief or economic reconstruction programmes (see Figure I). The remainder is **multilateral aid**, given to organisations such as the United Nations. This will then be used by the UN in their work with countries throughout the world.

The Swedish International Development Authority (SIDA) is responsible for the majority of the country's bilateral aid. Sweden gives aid to the world's poorest countries, with the aim of reducing poverty and promoting long-term sustainable development. Most is donated to countries in Africa and Asia (see Figure J).

Other government agencies provide technical and financial assistance to developing countries. Since 1990, Sweden has been one of the countries providing assistance to the countries of central and eastern Europe. Since 1990, the Swedish government has financed nearly 200 projects, mostly in Poland and the Baltic States.

The Swedish government contributes approximately $450 million per year to multilateral aid. The majority of this is given to the United Nations, although since joining the European Union in 1995 Sweden has allocated 10 % of its aid budget to the EU. In addition, there are estimated to be over 300 non-government organisations in Sweden providing development assistance to poorer countries, primarily in the areas of health and education.

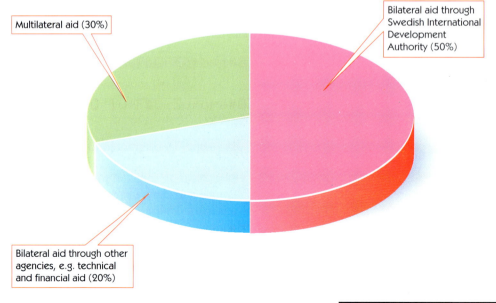

Multilateral aid (30%)

Bilateral aid through Swedish International Development Authority (50%)

Bilateral aid through other agencies, e.g. technical and financial aid (20%)

Figure I   Swedish development aid

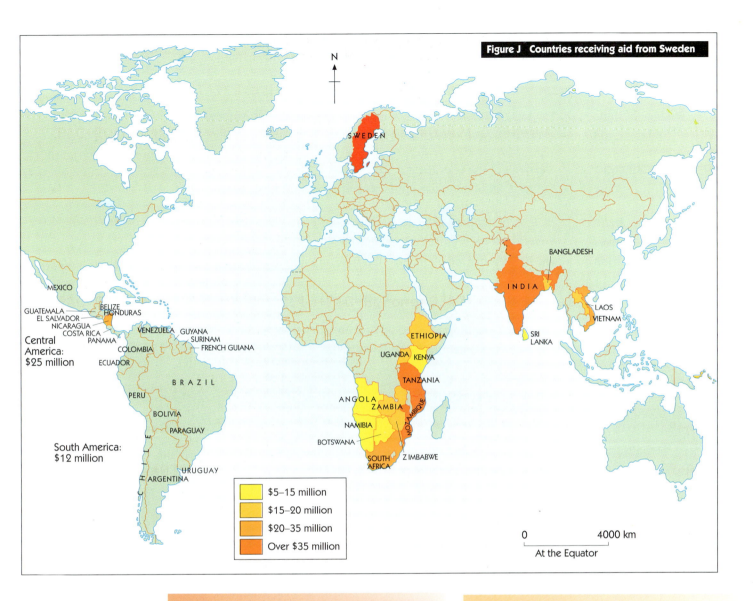

Central America: $25 million

South America: $12 million

$5–15 million
$15–20 million
$20–35 million
Over $35 million

0   4000 km
At the Equator

▼ Questions

Look at Figure H, showing overseas development aid given by industrialised countries.

1 Choosing a suitable technique, illustrate each of the sets of figures.

2 Describe what the figures show about development aid.

3 Which of the two sets of figures do you think gives a more accurate picture of aid given by rich countries? Give reasons for your answer.

4 Can you think of any other ways in which development aid could be measured?

5 'Rich countries have a moral duty to give aid to poorer nations. It is not right that most of the world's wealth is owned by a minority of its population, and some of the western world's prosperity has come from exploiting poorer countries in the first place.'

Write about what you think of this statement, using specific examples.

Review

The European Union is the world's leading trading power. The majority of the EU's external trade is with industrialised countries, such as Japan and the USA. The EU operates a trading deficit with these nations, and a surplus with developing nations.

Industrialised countries provide development aid for developing nations. This may be in the form of official government aid, or through charities and other non-government organisations. The EU is the largest provider of overseas development aid in the world. Aid may bring problems as well as benefits to the recipient countries. Sweden, as one of Europe's wealthiest nations, provides nearly 1 % of its GNP each year to overseas development aid.

Glossary

B

Balance of trade — The total value of a country's imports compared to its exports. *91*

Bilateral aid — Aid that is given by a country and is allocated to a specific country. *94*

C

Camargue — The delta of the river Rhône. *20*

Core — A central and most prosperous area of economic development. *63*

D

Delta — An area of material deposited at the mouth of a river. *26*

Dikes — A mound of earth raised to prevent flooding. *26*

Desertification — The transformation of once productive land into desert. *20*

E

Ecosystem — A system that shows the relationships between a community of living things (plants and animals) and their non-living environment. *43*

Europoort — The world's leading port, occupying 25 kilometres to the west of Rotterdam. *30*

Eutrophication — The over-enrichment of water by nutrients, leading to an excess of water-plants and animals. *17*

F

Fjords — A long, narrow rock-bound inlet. *23*

Fluvio-glacial material — Material carried by streams flowing from rivers. *10*

G

Globalisation — The production and sale of commodities on a world-wide basis. *54*

Gneiss — A coarse grained metamorphic rock, usually composed of quartz, feldspar and mica. *9*

Granite — A coarse grained igneous rock composed of quartz, feldspar and mica. *9*

H

Hamlet — A cluster of houses in the country. *35*

Hydro-electric power — Electricity produced by means of water power. *10*

I

International trade — The exchange of goods, commodities and services between countries. *91*

Invisible trade — Trade involving services. *91*

M

Multilateral aid — Aid given by a country to international organisations, such as the United Nations. This will then be used in countries throughout the world. *94*

P

Periphery — An outer and least prosperous area of economic development. *63*

Polder — An area of reclaimed land which is mainly surrounded by raised dikes, within which water levels can be controlled. *27*

R

Renewable — May be used more than once. *23*

S

Species — Living organisms which can breed with each other. *20*

Subsidies — A grant of public money in aid of an industry. *43*

Sustainable — A resource which may be used without the long term depletion of that resource. *23*

T

Trade deficit — Where the cost of a country's imports exceeds the value of its exports. *91*

Trade surplus — Where a country earns more than the cost of its imports. *91*

Transnational — A company with production and sales in more than one country. *47*

V

Visible trade — Trade involving goods and commodities. *91*

W

Wetland — Marshy areas which are a habitat for wildlife. *20*